BUDDHA

BOOKS BY WALTER HENRY NELSON

History and Biography
THE BERLINERS: Their City and Their Saga
THE LONDONERS: Life in a Civilised City
THE SOLDIER KINGS: The House of Hohenzollern
GERMANY REARMED
HEMINGWAY ANECDOTES

Business and Economics
SMALL WONDER: The Amazing Story of the Volkswagen
THE GREAT DISCOUNT DELUSION
THE ECONOMIC WAR AGAINST THE JEWS
(co-authored by Terence Prittie)

Fiction
THE SIEGE OF BUCKINGHAM PALACE

Frontispiece: Mucalinda Buddha. Prah Kham, Cambodia.
Sandstone, 12th Century CE.

BUDDHA

His Life and His Teaching

WALTER HENRY NELSON

Jeremy P. Tarcher/Putnam
a member of
Penguin Putnam Inc.
New York

Most Tarcher/Putnam books are available at special quantity discounts for bulk pur-
chase for sales promotions, premiums, fund-raising, and educational needs. Special
books or book excerpts also can be created to fit specific needs. For details, write Putnam Special Markets, 375 Hudson Street, New York, NY 10014.

Jeremy P. Tarcher/Putnam
a member of
Penguin Putnam Inc.
375 Hudson Street
New York, NY 10014
www.penguinputnam.com

Originally published in Great Britain under the title
Gautama Buddha by Luzac Oriental
First trade paperback edition 2000

Library of Congress Cataloging-in-Publication Data

Nelson, Walter Henry.
[Gautama Buddha]
Buddha : his life and his teaching / Walter Henry Nelson.
p.   cm.
Originally published: Gautama Buddha. London : Luzac Oriental, 1996.
Includes bibliographical references and index.
ISBN 1-58542-001-8
1. Gautama Buddha.   2. Gautama Buddha—Teachings.   3. Buddhists—India—
Biography.   I. Title.
BQ882.N45   2000   99-041849 CIP
294.3'63—dc21
[B]

Printed in the United States of America
1   3   5   7   9   10   8   6   4   2

This book is printed on acid-free paper. ∞

For Samantha Christine

Contents

Foreword

*T*HE BUDDHA WAS A MAN. However extraordinary he was, however much myth and legend have attributed supernatural powers to him, he was a human and not a divine being. He was "a man self-perfected, one who had achieved the mind's enlightenment," as one Buddhist put it.[1] His teaching, transmitted orally at first and written down well after his death, explained the way towards such enlightenment; it has therefore often been regarded as psychology as much as the religion-philosophy which it came to be called.

Because the Buddha was a self-perfected man, he is of interest to all who search beyond materialism for a goal in life, and for a way towards attaining that goal. It is no matter whether it can be reached; the journey is worthwhile and may, indeed, be the goal itself. Nor does it matter whether one's questions are fully answered, for questions have always been of greater importance than any answers we are offered; indeed, it is in the question itself that we may find the answer we seek.

In our modern Western world we are as drowned in ready answers as we are starved of real questions. Indeed, such questioning is mocked, especially by those "intellectual sophisticates" who deride the search for Truth and Meaning; all too often, we are invited to participate in a materialistic, consumerist life whose moral injunction is "Shop 'till you drop!" and which urges us to confuse change with growth, "progress" with development. "Pigs for more pigs for more pigs," describes an economic view of "a world of frenzied producers [which] requires as its complement a world of frenzied consumers."[2]

Despite this, many of us recognise the absurdity and horror of living only to work more, so as to earn more in order to spend more; the absurdity of finding meaning for our lives in a universe proclaimed to be without any ultimate meaning and purpose, and an aim in a life which we are cynically advised is aimless. It is to such people that this book is offered.

As the bibliography shows, there exists a wealth of books about Buddhism – indeed, far more than are included in that listing. Many are more academic than my own exploration of Buddha and Buddhism; while some seem speculative, scholastic or argumentative, there are others imbued with the understanding of writers who have penetrated deeply into the meaning of the Dhamma, the teaching of the Buddha. My own effort, meant as an introduction for the general reader, derives from my respect for Buddhism and the great traditional religions.

Buddhism itself developed into many forms since the Buddha died almost 500 years before the birth of Christ. Countless elaborate supernatural accretions involving Indian deities have transformed a simple if profound story of one man's struggle for self-perfection into an elaborate, complex, although often beautiful and charming, religious myth. These ancient legends, some of which are included here, are meant to evoke awe and inspire devotion, but the modern reader of course does not need to accept as literally true the feats of strength attributed to the Prince Siddhartha, for example, or the occasional intercessions of the gods to smooth the way for Gautama in his journey to enlightenment.

Over the centuries, many Buddhist schools and sects have come into being, as often as not related to those religions Buddhism encountered in the lands it penetrated; in Tibet, for example, it was married to forms derived from the country's ancient Bön religion, as well as to Hindu Tantric practices. That was inevitable; no matter, for the light of the Buddha and his original teaching, the *Dhamma*, shines also in these, as it does so profoundly in the Zen Buddhism of Japan. It is my hope that it may also shine through these pages.

Acknowledgements

MOST DEEPLY I AM INDEBTED to the late Christmas Humphreys who, while president of The Buddhist Society, London, of which he was the founder, read and commented upon a draft of this book; his encouraging letters, in which he expressed a liking of my fledgling effort, emboldened me to continue, while his own masterly books on Buddhism set an example as inspirational as impossible to emulate. Without his early encouragement, my book would certainly never have been completed or seen the light of day.

I am indebted to others as well, although it should of course be noted that only I can be held responsible for any shortcomings the book has. In New York, I was assisted in my research by William Stablein and received encouragement from Tibetan scholars as well as Buddhists prominent in delegations to the United Nations. In London, I was encouraged by Jeffrey and Nobuko Somers, and assisted editorially by my friends Ann Caplowe and Roy Ashwell. The interest and patience shown by Laurent and Susan Lacroix is also most appreciated.

Quotation from the following works is respectfully acknowledged: Edward J. Thomas, *The Life of Buddha as Legend and History* (London: Routledge & Kegan Paul, 1927; paperback, 1975); D. W. Rhys Davids, *Buddhist Suttas* (N.Y.: Dover Publications, 1969); Christmas Humphreys, *Buddhism* (London: Penguin Books, 1951); J.-M. Dechanet, OSB, *Christian Yoga* (New York: Harper & Brothers, 1960); A. R. Orage, *The Active Mind* (N.Y.: Hermitage House, 1954).

Photographs are from the collection of the Library of the Gurdjieff Society, London. Copyrights of these photos remain unknown and are being sought. The cover illustration, of the baby

Buddha, or Prince Siddhartha Gautama as an infant, is from the collection of Mr and Mrs Jeffrey Somers, and is an ink painting by Sochu Suzuki, Zen Abbot of the Ryutakuji Temple, Mishima, Japan.

BUDDHA

Look upon the world as a bubble, look upon it as a
mirage: the king of death does not see him who
thus looks down upon the world.
Come, look at the glittering world, like unto a royal
chariot; the foolish are immersed in it, but the
wise do not cling to it.

The Dhammapada (v. 170–71)

I

The Land Awaits

OUR DAWN LIES SHROUDED IN mystery. Recorded history goes
back only a few thousand years. Of a time before that, we only
know that civilisations prospered in ways unknown and died in
ways that remain obscure.

One such civilisation, thousands of years before the birth of
Christ, lay in India. Of it, there remain a few shards – and our
wonder. To look at its traces is to look upon the land in which the
Buddha came to be born.

The time is 2300 BCE.*

Throughout the Middle and Far East, people create marvels.
On the Nile, they build the first pyramid; in Mesopotamia, the
Hanging Gardens of Babylon; and throughout the regions in
which such new activity represents a flowering of culture, people
search to understand the reasons for their existence and place in
the universe.

These are no "primitive" people, but individuals with a complex and ordered society: inventive, technically proficient, able to
communicate both mathematics and metaphysics in written form.

---

* Because it seems appropriate here to use non-Christian designations for dates, BCE
("Before the Common Era") is used throughout, instead of BC ("Before Christ"); similarly, CE
(for "of the Common Era") is used instead of AD (Anno Domini, or "In the Year of Our Lord").

16

In India, they resided, as far as we know, at Harappa and Mohenjo-Dara, in the north-west of the vast Indian subcontinent. There may well have been other cities of what we call the Harappan – or Indus Valley – civilisation, but they are lost. Nor do we even know the people of these two towns. Who they were, what they looked like, and how they vanished, remains a mystery.

The towns they built, each three miles in circumference, are impressive. Like the peoples of the mysterious civilisation of Cnossus which vanished in the Aegean Sea so long ago that even the ancient Romans marvelled at its antiquity, the Harappans practised advanced arts and crafts, had baths in most homes, and even public drainage systems.

Each city contained a citadel, built on a high spot overlooking the life of the town; in these were palaces, halls, baths, and storage places for grain. Streets were straight, met at right angles, and were laid out with care. The homes which flanked the streets were connected to a sewage system; irrigation ditches and canals existed as well.

The people of this Indus Valley produced ornaments and implements of considerable beauty; even terra cotta toys for Harappan children have been found. There was a system of counting and measuring, as well as a system of writing, not yet deciphered for no Harappan "Rosetta Stone" has been unearthed.

These undeciphered characters read from right to left and, on the next line, from left to right, and so on down the page – back and forth in a system of writing called Boustrophedon. It must have been a syllabic script, for it contains 396 signs, too many for a proper alphabet. There were accent marks too, suggesting that the people of the Indus Valley were advanced in their pronunciations. Perhaps some of the script dealt with Harappan commerce, for there are signs that the peoples of these two towns were merchants and traders, even in touch with the distant Mesopotamian civilisation as long ago as 2350 BCE.

Perhaps not only trade flowed between India and Mesopotamia and between India and Persia, with which the Harappans were also in touch, but also the more important commodity of ideas.

Travellers – the merchants of the caravans and perhaps ambassadors and priests – may well have stimulated the exchange of
thoughts about the nature of the universe and our place and purpose in it.

What ideas the Harappans may have had regarding such
questions is uncertain. The signs they left behind suggest they
worshipped a Great Mother or Earth Goddess, followed a fertility
cult, and that certain animals and trees were sacred to them.
Among the latter was the pipal tree which many centuries later
would again be revered by others, for it would be beneath such a
tree that Prince Siddhartha Gautama would achieve enlightenment, from that day on to go about the world as the Buddha, the
Enlightened One.

Little else is known about the Harappan people – except that
they vanished around the seventeenth century BCE. We do not
know what they looked like, though some believe they may have
been Dravidians or ancestors of the Dravidians, an advanced
people who today inhabit the south of India.

It is now 1500 BCE and an event of great importance is about to
take place.

Through the north-west passes into India stream a new people,
fair-haired and blue-eyed, who call themselves *Aryas*, meaning
"noblemen" or "owners of land". We call them Aryans. Their
destiny was to rule and populate India and to bring to it their own
religion, a faith still followed in the subcontinent today.

Who were these people and from where did they emerge?

Again, we face the past with wonderment and awe. Much about
this strange people remains unknown. The Aryans may have orig-
inated in eastern Europe, near the Caspian Sea, and are believed
to have been a nomadic, inventive people who had domesticated
cattle and other animals, raised herds, and engaged in agriculture.
Thousands of years ago, for unknown reasons, they began to
move from their ancient homes, pack their belongings, form great

caravans, and march southward, westward, and eastward. There must have been vast numbers of them, organised in great tribes, for different groups of them settled in Persia and Greece, as well as in India.

Some crossed the mountains of Central Asia; others entered Iran, and an Indo-European or Aryan tribe called the Hellenes became the ancestors of the ancient Greeks. They spoke a language which today is the root-language of almost all European tongues. Sanskrit was the language they brought to India; it is closely connected with many European languages and, again, demonstrates the inter-relationship. The Sanskrit *matr*, for example, came to be *mater* in Latin, *Mütter* in German, and *mother* in English; it came to be *moder* in Swedish, *madre* in Portuguese, Spanish, and Italian, and *mat* in Russian.

Just how the Aryans entered the Indian subcontinent we do not know. They probably entered it in waves rather than in one organised "army", though they were indeed prepared to defend themselves and conquer; they rode horses, wore armour, and carried bows and arrows. They had leaders and organisation. According to their own records (the *Vedas*), they encountered, battled, and subdued a primitive brown-skinned Indian people, for whom they apparently had little respect. Were these the Harappans? They may have been, if the Harappans were the ancestors of the Dravidians, for these latter people were indeed dark-complexioned. Yet neither the Harappans nor the Dravidians could objectively be called "primitive" or justifiably be regarded with superior contempt. Also, in order to "meet" the Harappans, some conflict of dates would have to be resolved, for it is believed the Aryans entered India around 1500 BCE, while the fall of Harappa and Mohenjo-Dara is dated at two centuries earlier. Of course, all dates so long ago are perforce inexact and it may well be that the Aryans caused the fall of these two civilisations in battle. Perhaps their air of superiority was caused only by their notion of themselves as mighty conquerors, as victors in the struggle. Traces of a conflagration at Harappa have been discovered and it may, indeed, have been burnt down by an Aryan tribe.

If, however, Harappa and Mohenjo-Dara no longer existed in 1500 BCE, then the invading Aryans must have fought others indigenous to the region. We know that there were also truly primitive peoples in India, who later sought refuge in the forests, and it may have been these whom the Aryans came upon.

They settled down to stay.

They were not an urban people and did not choose to build cities. They lived close to the soil, in small villages, and it was not to be for centuries that the great cities of India would be built.

For the time being, the Aryans lived a simple life and went to some lengths to preserve their traditions and perhaps also to keep from being intermixed with the indigenous peoples of India. Gradually, this effort developed into a formal "caste system".

The Aryans remained in the northern part of India and, even by 800 BCE, never penetrated past the centre of the subcontinent, to which they had pressed the Dravidians. Perhaps they did not even know how vast was the region they had entered. The land stretched two thousand miles from north to south and almost another two thousand from east to west.

Its name derived from the Greek word *Indos*, an adaptation of the Persian *hindu*, meaning "land of the great river". In Sanskrit, the language of the Aryans, "river" is *sindhu* – again showing the closeness of the Sanskrit, Persian, and Greek words. They form the root of both the name of the Indian nation and of the Hindu peoples themselves, whose common language today is Hindi.

It was in Sanskrit that the Aryans first wrote down their religion, in a series of texts called the Vedas. This transcription took place around 500 BCE, but the faith was hundreds – probably thousands – of years older, passed by word of mouth from sage to sage, from *guru* (teacher or master) to guru. There are four Vedas, of which the first, the *Rig Veda*, is regarded as the most significant; the others are the *Yajur*, *Sama*, and *Atharva Vedas*. The Vedas are in India considered eternal, uncreated, and incontestable scripture, though subject to interpretation. While they form the written teaching, in India all teaching is and has always been orally transmitted and the guidance of a guru is considered indispensable.

The Vedas reveal that the Aryans brought to India a system of gods, the chief of whom was Indra. World creation and the forces of nature were explained in the Vedas and there was sun worship, a form of fire worship. The religion was anthropomorphic, the gods having human attributes, and fire was regarded as the connection between the gods and men.

Mantras (prayers) and other invocations, including sacrifices and elaborate rituals, abounded; inevitably, this meant that priests proliferated. After a time, commentaries were added to the Vedas; these explained in complex form how worship was to be carried out and helped further to fix the role of the Vedic priests. Called *Brahmanas*, these commentaries led to a religion referred to as Brahmanism.

Brahman is a word with many meanings. In one form, *bráhman* means "prayer", while in another, *brahmán*, it means "he who prays" (pray-er). *Brahmanaspati* became the Lord of Prayer and priests came to be called *Brahmans*. As for the word "*Brahma*" itself, it represents the ultimate, absolute, universal, creative deity – "God" in the most abstract form.

Brahmanism eventually was to provide the world with two of the greatest Indian religious works, the *Upanishads* and the *Bhagavad Gita*. Sublime in thought and language, they belong to the great literature of all times and peoples. Mystical works of great philosophical and spiritual importance, they address themselves to the fundamental questions of the universe.

Over the centuries, however, the Vedic faith became increasingly sophisticated, in the sense that it became more and more difficult to comprehend, filled with magic, incantations, strata and substrata of symbolism. Few outside the priestly orders were taught anything regarding it and those on the bottom or near-bottom of the social scale were left to worship either primitive, pre-Aryan nature gods and other deities, or to consider only the outer shell of the Brahmanic faith, without ever approaching its inner, more symbolic meaning.

Only Aryans were allowed to follow the Brahmanic faith and only the top layers of the Aryans were allowed to approach its meaning – and its temples. Partly in order to protect themselves from intermixture with non-Aryans and partly to provide their priests with special status, the Aryans developed the caste system based on occupation more than anything else.

At the top was a spiritual aristocracy, the priests, forming the Brahman caste, though not all in that caste were necessarily priests, some for example being senior officials and counsellors to kings. Below them were the *Kshatriyas*, rulers and warriors, and below them the *Vaisyas*, merchants and other commoners. The lowest caste consisted of *Sudras*, serfs, but even further below them were the *Panchamas*, a group who were literally out-castes.

The three topmost castes formed the upper layer of the Aryan culture; its male members wore the "sacred thread", given them in a special initiation ceremony as boys, signifying their "second birth". Movement from one caste to another was out of the question and intermarriage between castes was forbidden, except that a higher-caste male could marry a lower-caste female. Yet it is important to recognise that Indians saw this caste system as perfectly natural; it is only in recent years that it has come to be frowned upon. In today's India, laws "abolish" both castes and out-castes ("untouchables"), but the customs of thousands of years cannot so easily be erased.

In actuality, there are more than the four "main" castes listed – perhaps as many as two thousand may be said to exist! Within each of the main four castes, there are members who will look up to others within their caste, and look down upon still others. A high-caste Brahman from one section of the subcontinent might actually find himself snubbed in another part of the land, where his particular "branch" of the Brahman caste is considered inferior. Also, Indians tend to create new "castes" with as much avidity as Westerners create fraternal orders or clubs: some years ago, two thousand Indians who decided to start smoking formed a "smokers' caste".

Indians justify the caste system partly on the basis of their belief in rebirth. According to this, a child is born into a higher or lower caste according to the merits acquired by it in a previous life. Someone who performs conscientiously his role in the present life has hopes of being reborn into better circumstances in the next; at the same time, what misfortune befalls him in this life he regards as a clear effect of neglected duties in a previous incarnation.

Thus the present life is the effect of the past one as well as the cause of the next, and the law governing this – that of *karma* or, roughly, that of cause-and-effect – is seen as just, universal, and inescapable.

The caste system did much to remove the Brahmanic faith from the reality of the life of those at the bottom of the ladder. Denied access to certain temples, denied instruction, and kept rigidly apart from the higher castes, millions of low-caste Indians were kept in ignorance and spiritual emptiness. By the time of the Buddha's birth, around 600 BCE, the Brahman priesthood had become a rigid, often corrupt, and exclusive society, in private communion with their gods.

It is now the sixth century before Christ. Brahmanism is over 900 years old in India, a complex and secret teaching foreign to those whose lot it is to work humbly on the soil.

The land is rich and fertile, not yet over-populated. Villages prosper and support the towns. Life is as it has always been: those who till the fields and tend the animals follow the occupations of their fathers and will teach their sons the same. Blacksmiths, potters, and carpenters – all hereditary occupations – make the tools the village needs; they and other craftsmen such as silversmiths and oilseed pressers are paid in crops by the villagers they serve. The villagers have little to do with outsiders; they support themselves and need only pay their princes or kings a portion of their produce, in taxes. These rulers, in turn, pass on a portion to the more powerful lords whom they serve. Generally, the people are content and well-treated by their lords; through village councils, they even have a measure of democracy.

There is little excitement in the air. The heat, combined with the stagnant priestly society, produces a peaceful, slumbering land. Mechanically, people follow their allotted tasks and the customs of ancient days. They are drowsy and the land sleeps.

Soon, however, they will be awakened. For a giant who shall shake them has been born.

The baby Buddha, or Prince Siddhartha Gautama as an infant by
Sochu Suzuki, Zen Abbot of the Ryutakuji Temple, Mishima, Japan.

A supernatural person is not easily found, he is not born everywhere. Wherever such a sage is born, that race prospers.

The Dhammapada (v. 193)

II

The Two Roads

LUMBINI PARK, NEAR MADEIRA, FORMERLY Kapilavastu. Before us King Asoka's pillar, erected in 239 BCE. We read the inscription: *Here was the Enlightened One born.*

Kapilavastu lies in the north of Gorakhpur district, west of the Indian state of Bihar and south of the land of Nepal. It is in north-eastern India, within sight of the great Himalayas.

What occurred then in Lumbini Park took place in the year 563 BCE. It is said to have been the last of the Buddha's births.

Man is born, grows, withers, dies; he lives, loves and laments; he rejoices in manhood, suffers in ailment and adversity, bends down in old age and falls in death – all this we know. Yet here, in India, they teach of transmigration, and of the Wheel of Life which symbolises this rebirth. Round and round this symbolic wheel turns inexorably and, on each revolution, reaches again birth and again death. Thus it is that human beings die only to be reborn, and are born only to face again the inevitable cycle of growth, enfeeblement and death; of life, love and lamentation. This wheel is like a spiral, turning upwards and downwards, and it is each person's task to raise themselves during each life until the top may possibly be reached. Thus living becomes an exercise of the spirit, with each life imbued with great meaning, and life is a gymnasium in which all may perfect themselves. Ultimately, even the lowest, through great efforts, can be raised – or through their lack be assured an endless repetition of the life-cycle, in a spiritual involution.

Those who have evolved and liberated themselves from the turning of the wheel are regarded as Perfected Ones. It is said of them that, through countless lives of spiritual striving, they have cut the chains which bind them to this wheel and, at the most, have only one or two more lives to live.

The Buddha, we are told, was one such man. It is said that in the heavenly zones, where great souls wait out the span of 30,000 years before they must again be born, the Buddha knew his time had come.

"The earth suffers," he said, "and I shall come to help this one last time before the law of birth and rebirth stops for me."

As fit vessels for his incarnation, he chose King Suddhodana and his queen, the Lady Maya Diva, rulers of the Sakya (or Shakya) tribe at Kapilavastu. King Suddhodana's family name was Gautama, or Gotama.

The queen, legend has it, was so beautiful and pure that she had been named Maya, meaning "illusion" or "illusory", for her extraordinary beauty seemed the stuff of dreams. She had, according to legend, taken a vow of chastity, one which the pious king respected. And so it was that she, like Mary, 563 years later, was reputably a virgin when she bore the Illumined One.

This "virgin birth" of the Buddha* is one of the many legends surrounding his life. Believing in them is not a requirement for those who respond to the truths the Buddha proclaimed; they belong here to allow us to savour the East's wonder at the life of this great teacher.

Another legend reports the Lady Maya telling her husband one morning of a dream she had during the night. Such a report would have been received with gravity, for dreams were believed to be one of the ways in which the gods communicated with mortals.

---

* More accurately, then of the Boddhisattva, literally "awakening being", someone who aspires to become a Buddha. It was 35 years later that he, having become the "awakened one", was called the Buddha.

"How strange, my lord," she said to King Suddhodana. "Last night I dreamed that, as I lay upon my bed, the Four Rulers of the World took up my cot and transported me to the great Himalayas, to set me down upon a mountaintop. There, a great, many-tusked white elephant came towards me and touched me on the side with his trunk, and I was filled with bliss. What can this dream portend, what can its meaning be?"

King Suddhodana summoned those who read the meanings of such dreams, the dream-readers of the palace, skilled astrologers and wise men, who listened to the queen's tale with awe and wonder.

"The dream is good!" they said.
"The Crab is in conjunction with the Sun;
The Queen shall bear a boy, a holy child
Of wondrous wisdom, profiting all flesh,
Who shall deliver men from ignorance,
Or rule the world, if he will deign to rule."[3]

Great king and conqueror, then, would the child be – or a great sage.

King Suddhodana rejoiced, for he had waited anxiously for the birth of a son who might succeed him as ruler of his people. As was then not unusual, the king was married to two women, both to the Lady Maya and to her sister, the Lady Japiti, sometimes referred to as Mahaprajapati, yet he still had no heir. The birth that was expected therefore caused as much wonder as joy, for the child's mother was to be the virgin queen and not her sister.

When the day approached on which the Buddha was to be born, the two sister-queens left Kapilavastu to return home to their own father, a neighbouring ruler, to have the birth take place within his palace. On this journey, Queen Maya realised the birth was imminent; halting at Lumbini Park, she lay down beneath a sandalwood tree as straight as a temple pillar, upon a bed of flowers. Thus it was that the Lord Buddha was born simply, upon the earth, during a journey's halt, in much the same manner as Jesus of Nazareth would be born centuries later.

The legends say that, at the moment of his birth, there were heavenly signs which told the wise men that a Buddha had been born. To the north, in the Himalayan mountains, where Indian holy men led hermit lives of meditation and asceticism, the Great Sage Asita marvelled at the wondrous signs. Divining the reasons, he is said to have transported himself miraculously through the air to the court of Kapilavastu.

The queen and her new-born son had returned and Asita begged permission to see the baby boy. The child had been named Siddhartha, meaning "he who has achieved his goal". Asita recognised on him the thirty-two overt signs of Buddhahood, as well as some eighty lesser marks upon his body, these being visible to him if not to others, thanks to his vision, wisdom and holiness.*

King Suddhodana and his queen tried to lay the new-born Prince Siddhartha at the sage's feet, to ask Asita's blessings upon the boy.

"Nay, not so!" Asita said, prostrating himself before the child. "He is the saviour, and I worship him."

Asita also confirmed a prophecy which had already been made by the palace's wise men: the boy will grow to be either the world's most powerful ruler or the world's saviour, mighty in either case and bringing honour to the Gautama name and the Sakya tribe.

Then Asita grew sad and wept, and when those in the court were troubled by his tears, asking whether they signified a misfortune which might befall the infant prince, the sage assured them that this was not the case. His eyes, he said, were filled with tears, for he knew that the child would, in manhood, most assuredly achieve Buddhahood, but that he, Asita, would not live to witness it or meet the Illumined One.

King Suddhodana grew troubled. It was not a large territory over which he ruled, yet his heart yearned for a son to succeed him as a king. India was in those days divided into countless small principalities and kingdoms, each governed by a noble who in

* Signs also traditionally those of a "great man", one who might become either a saint or a great ruler. See "Signs of" in Glossary.

turn pledged his loyalty to an even mightier king. In the case of the Sakyas, Suddhodana bowed before the ruler of Kosala.

But the king's fears were still new and vague; they would visit him more powerfully in the years to come. In the meantime, his heart was saddened just one short week after the prince's birth had made it glad.

Queen Maya died seven days after the birth. Her earthly task, said the wise men, had been completed and her purity and piety now set her free of the wheel of life.

The young prince was given over to the Lady Japiti, to be raised by her. According to legend, at the moment of Queen Maya's death, Japiti's breasts swelled with sweet milk for the young prince, a miracle which showed the gods' concern for the child.

The prince must have had a happy, carefree childhood, for young nobles led lives full of luxury and ease and play. In his later years, the Buddha spoke of these days of his early youth, of the silks and jewels he wore and the servants who attended him. He played with the children of the courtiers and with his cousins, roaming the palace buildings and the large walled gardens in which were all possible delights.

The king watched the young child at play and in his heart was pleasure at the prince's carefree ways; still there remained a silent fear that the boy might one day be led to live the religious life.

The king was not a worldly man and never failed to honour those who had chosen to become ascetics. Yet he feared, understandably, for the continuance of his kingly line and for his subjects too. He wished to see them governed by a Gautama prince, by the fair Siddhartha, who even in his younger years showed unmistakable signs of a fine character. Ever ready to serve, he was clearly prepared to rule; deferential towards his superiors and compassionate and loving towards those beneath him in rank, he was loved by all.

And it was for these reasons that Suddhodana feared his son's departure from the world of kings.

India was filled with holy men, ascetics, and mendicant monks. It was highly regarded to give up the illusory world of temporal allurements and to venture into the forest, wearing the coarsest and simplest garb and carrying only a begging bowl. One meal a day was all these ascetics asked, stopping at the doors of village homes to receive their offering of food, usually a small portion of rice. They were not looked upon as beggars, and it was virtually unheard of for anyone to turn them away or to refuse them. Any home was honoured by the visit of a monk and the offering given him brought merit to the donor.

From earliest childhood, high-caste Indians of the day were taught that the most worthy aim in an individual's life is to perfect himself spiritually. All else, even the joys of parenthood and the bliss of an harmonious marriage, paled before this great and golden aim. A man or woman who pursued "life aims" only, making a living, raising a family, had wasted their span of life, if the needs of the spirit were ignored. The world was "Maya" – illusion – and reality lay only in the great truths embodied in the Vedas and the Brahmanas, in sacrifice and worship, and in the resulting perfecting of man's nature.

Great numbers of Indians, therefore left the world of struggle, craving, and illusion to pursue the harsher disciplines of the ascetic life. Indeed, in those days, asceticism had reached an almost destructive pitch; the belief of many was that spiritual enlightenment could come only after the fires of the body were almost totally extinguished. Monks often brought themselves to a state of near-death, undergoing terrible self-inflicted hardships, in the hope of overcoming the demands which the bodily "envelope" of the soul constantly made. They believed the organism had to be silenced and the calls it made upon the consciousness had to be virtually extinguished, before Pure Spirit could be approached.

This was a common belief then and, in his adult life, the Buddha would have much to say about it.

The ascetics and monks of the day did not belong to a monastic order; there were no buildings such as monasteries and no organisation, complete with abbot, to govern their lives. Those who did not live in larger groups with their teachers, or gurus, lived for the most part alone or in small groups, in forests, by roadsides, or in mountain caves, pursuing lives of meditation dedicated to the perfection of their souls, through the most rigorous mental and physical self-disciplines. Often, they were by birth high-caste Brahmans, for the Brahmanic ideal even today is for a man of this caste to inhabit four stages of life.

First, in childhood, he would be a student; then, in manhood, he would marry, raise a family, and pursue his worldly life-goal. In this second stage, depending upon the caste and family tradition into which he had been born, he might serve as a ruler, a soldier, or a merchant. In the third stage of life, as his years had ripened, he would pass on to others the accumulated knowledge and understanding of his years, and would teach for the benefit of the young. Finally, in the fourth stage of a man's life, he would abandon all and seek his own self-perfection through the way of the ascetic and wandering monk.

Kings and nobles paid great heed to wise men and, without doubt, King Suddhodana would have had several reside with him inside the palace grounds, perhaps within the palace buildings themselves or in huts in the palace gardens. But while he respected them, he did not wish the Prince Siddhartha to join their ranks. Perhaps he felt that there would be time for that; Siddhartha should pursue this path late in his life, after spending his active years ruling the Sakya peoples wisely and well.

His fears were also based upon the "worldly" aspect of the prophecy the wise men had pronounced. What an honour it would be for the Sakya people, what lustre for the family of Gautama, if this prince, Siddhartha, were indeed to become the mightiest ruler on earth, before whom all other kings and princes bowed!

And so, one day early in Siddhartha's life, the king called his wise men, sages, and ministers to council.

Into his chamber they came, obedient to the royal call. They gazed upon the face of King Suddhodana and saw that it was troubled. He was, then, not calling them for the accustomed reasons, to discuss some verse of the Vedas which puzzled him, or to hear the wisest of them discourse on the tales of the god Indra.

Had some messenger brought to their king news of political ferment? Were the Sakya soldiers to be called out, were ambassadors to be dispatched to some hostile king, and were they now summoned to determine how most subtly to phrase the kingly letters?

King Suddhodana waited until all were seated, cross-legged, before him. And then he spoke.

"You who have counselled me in all these years gone by, counsel me now with all your wisdom! Offer the sacrifices that are necessary and let us recite the mantras that are seemly to this occasion. I need words which come from the depth of your wisdom, summoned from the storehouse of your understanding, and born of your experience in this and other lives, today made ready for the king's wish and command.

"You have meditated upon the meaning of our queen's dream, when she conceived the Prince Siddhartha. You have given me the meaning of that dream. You and I have heard the sage Asita, he who dwells in the Himalayan heights, confirm its meaning. The Prince Siddhartha is to become the greatest ruler of men the world has seen, a conqueror noble and mighty, respected by all and feared by his enemies. He is to bring glory to our Sakya peoples and brilliance to the Gautama line. His manhood will illumine our race and of him will be spoken as far as mankind dwells, even to those lands of legend, where the setting sun sinks into the waters and not the land.

"This shall the Prince Siddhartha be, if you can help. For there is another prophecy yet, that he shall leave our land leaderless upon my death, cast off his princely robes, refuse the throne and duties he was born to assume – to enter the forests as a ragged monk, as a self-starved ascetic, as a holy man whose purpose is the perfection of his soul.

"Wise men and ministers and honoured friends, counsel me! Tell me how the Prince Siddhartha may be stayed from this path, the path of renunciation, at least until he has reached old age, when it is meet and seemly that he spend his last remaining years in seeking self-perfection. What prayers can you utter, what rites and incantations perform, what gods invoke, what magic bring to bear to ease this burden which weighs upon my heart?"

Suddhodana waited for the wise men to reply. For a long while, the chamber was silent and the air heavy with expectancy. The wise men probed their hearts in meditation; single-pointedly, they concentrated their attention on an answer to the king's grave question.

Finally, one of them spoke. He was the oldest among them and therefore the most respected. He looked at the others and divined their answers: theirs were the same as his.

"Oh mighty king !" he said. "The Prince Siddhartha will indeed be the mighty ruler of whom you spoke – if but one thing may be arranged."

King Suddhodana leaned forward intently.

"Yes, yes, what is it?" he asked, for he was ready to make all arrangements necessary, issue all the orders that might be needed, and have the king's word passed that this and that be done, whatever the wise men said. Such was the king's pious regard for his holy sages.

"He must be kept," the aged counsellor said, "from ever seeing these signs of human suffering: old age and the decrepitude thereof, sickness and the way it lays waste the body, and death. If this be done, he shall be well-content and will not ask the meaning of the life he leads, but will just lead it. Yet his spirit is so gentle and so all-compassionate that, should he see these signs of human suffering, he will be quite unable to ignore them and will perforce leave behind the world of kings and princes."

If the prince were to see four signs – a sick man, an old man, a corpse, and an ascetic – then, said another of the wise men, he would renounce the world.

Guards were posted at the four quarters of the palace, to ensure that no one bearing these four signs could be encountered by the prince. And so Siddhartha's childhood was arranged, to pass amid beauty and pleasure only.

"I was delicate, O monks, extremely delicate, excessively delicate," the Buddha later told his followers, when he himself described the years of his youth and adolescence.[4]

"In my father's dwelling lotus-pools had been made, in one blue lotuses, in another red, in another white, all for my sake. I used no sandalwood that was not of Benares, my dress was of Benares cloth, my tunic, my under-robe, and cloak. Night and day a white parasol was held over me so that I should not be touched by cold or heat, by dust or weeds or dew.

"I had three palaces, one for the cold season, one for the hot, and one for the season of rains. Through the four rainy months, in the palace for the rainy season, entertained by female minstrels I did not come down from the palace; and as in the dwellings of others food from the husks of rice is given to the slaves and workmen together with sour gruel, so in my father's dwelling rice and meat was given to the slaves and workmen."

At the age of about eight, the education of the prince would have begun. While little is recorded of his childhood, we do know how the high-born have always been educated in India and have no reason for doubting this prince was taught in the same way.

Thus, at the age of eight, or nine, or ten, he would pass almost completely out of his family's dominion. His father, the king, would find a teacher to take him in charge. It was no small matter to find such a man. No doubt the wise men were consulted at great length, for the greatest sage of them all would be wanted. Finally, Viswamitra was the guru chosen.

In those legends of the Prince Siddhartha's life, in which his miraculous virgin birth is described, many other miraculous events take place.

There is the tale of Siddhartha's first meeting with Viswamitra.

The legend has it that the sage met the boy prince, who stood before him with eyes cast down, respectful before his teacher.

"Child, write this scripture," said the wise man, speaking the verse *Gayatri*, which only the high-born hear.

"Master, I write," Siddhartha said in deferential tones, and wrote, to the master's amazement:

> "Not in one script, but many characters,
> The sacred verse; Nagri and Dakshin, Ni,
> Mangal, Parusha, Yava, Tirthi, Uk,
> Darad, Sikhyani, Mana, Madhyachar,
> The pictured writings and the speech of signs,
> Tokens of cave-men and sea-peoples,
> Of those who worship snakes beneath the earth,
> And those who flames adore and the sun's orb,
> The Magians and the dwellers on the mounds;
> Of all the nations all strange scripts he traced
> One after other with his writing-stick,
> Reading the Master's verse in every tongue;
> And Viswamitra said, 'It is enough,
> Let us to numbers...'"[5]

In numbers too the boy is said to have confounded the sage, knowing the reckoning of every sum, how all the different orders of things of earth were counted, and after that, tested on measures, he knew the rule one takes to note the largest and the smallest, until he uttered to the sage the total of all atoms of the earth.

This Viswamitra heard upon his face, prostrate before the boy. "For thou," he cried, "art teacher of thy teachers – thou, not I, art guru. Oh, I worship thee, sweet prince! That comest to my school only to show thou knowest all without the books, and knowest fair reverence besides."[6]

Whether the lad did indeed miraculously know all, whether he could, as the legends would have us believe, recite all the sacred verses in all the tongues of earth, and whether he knew all sciences, is not important to us here. One thing stands out: the fairness of the prince's character, the beauty of his being.

Early he proved to be compassionate.

One day, the legends say, he was out hunting with his cousin Devadatta, that selfsame cousin who in later years would cause great mischief within the ranks of the Buddha's followers. Now, on this day, an arrow shot by Devadatta had pierced the wing of a swan, flying north with his fellows. The wounded bird fell at the feet of Prince Siddhartha.

Gently, Siddhartha picked the bird up, laid it upon his lap, and soothed its frightened and trembling body. With one hand, he held the swan, while with the other he carefully withdrew the barbed arrow from its wing, anointing the wound with cool leaves and healing honey.

"Prince Devadatta has shot down a swan," said a servant, running to Siddhartha, "and asks me to fetch it. Will you give it to me?"

Siddhartha gazed at the bird in his arms and shook his head.

"If it were dead, then I might do so," he said, "but the bird lives and is not my cousin's property."

Hearing Siddhartha's answer, Devadatta came, insisting, "Give me my prize, cousin! The bird belonged to no one in the sky, but once shot down, belongs to him who shot it."

Siddhartha held the frightened swan still closer. "If anyone's," he said, "the bird is mine by right of having healed it." Then, ever-considerate, he said to the scowling Devadatta, "Come, fair cousin, if you still insist, let us leave the judgement to the wise and both abide by the decision of the sages."

Devadatta agreed and the wise men met to deliberate. Some thought this and others that, and fine points of the law and ethics were discussed. Then, says the legend, an unknown priest stood up before the group and offered his opinion. "If life has value, then surely the saviour of that life owns it more than he who tried to kill it. For one sustains the life, while the other wastes it."

To this all agreed and the swan was given to Siddhartha. But when they sought to honour the strange priest and sent men after him, he could not be found. Some had seen him enter a temple but, within this, servants found only a hooded snake glide forth. All marvelled, for sometimes the gods came in such guises to men, appearing when needed, and then changing form.

The swan's wing healed and on a day a short while later, the bird flew north, to nest in the Himalayan peaks. Siddhartha watched it disappear and there was pain within his heart.

The growing boy learned other things beside the Vedas and the sciences. Sometimes, he asked his father to let him view the nearby towns, to see his Sakya people at their work, to learn how others lived, those he would someday rule.

The king, mindful of what the ministers and sages said, made careful preparation. Well in advance of Prince Siddhartha's entry into town or village, heralds would tell the townsfolk of King Suddhodana's commands:

"Water and sweep the streets and deck your homes and public places with silks and flowers! Remove all refuse and put on a festive air, so that the prince may gladden at your sight, returning to the palace with joy in his heart! The king commands that the infirm and old, and those with any blotch or blight, with marks or deformities, stay within doors. The king commands as well that on this day no bodies shall be burnt or funeral processions made and that all wailing for the dead shall be indoors, where doleful sounds cannot our prince's ears assail."

In his gaily painted wagon, drawn by two huge white steer, rode the Prince Siddhartha and no kingly commands were needed to make the people sing his praises or rejoice at his sight. For the growing lad was stately, handsome, and of such a sweet and gentle disposition as to radiate his goodness to all who watched.

The prince was gladdened by the happy sights he saw, but thoughtful too, for on some trips into the countryside, he had glimpsed other sides of life.

He noted in the fields how all things live to feed another, how creatures are born only to nourish other orders of beings, how the peasant sweated in the fields and how the bullocks strained; how crops were planted, grew, and were cut down, how life meant work and effort, not the ease and comfort of the palace courts.

Nor did he shrug these observations off, saying such was the nature of life on earth, but pondered what he saw, for he reasoned that behind all this lay some great cosmic laws, the nature of which he might some day divine. And so there grew in him a wonder about life, about its meaning, not just for him, but for the countless millions on this globe.

Frequently, the prince grew pensive and could be seen, sitting alone, cross-legged as the gurus sat, meditative, wondering and thoughtful.

The heart of his father grew heavy at that sight. Siddhartha, growing to manhood, would be thinking of the kind of life he was to lead.

"My son is learned and handsome and all regard him well," thought the king. "He sits his horse straight and firm and there are none in my kingdom who can ride as well, or shoot an arrow straighter at a target on the wall, nor are there youths as strong, as swift. Yet these things give him little pleasure and he sits distracted."

In this the king saw danger and, again, he summoned all his ministers and sages, describing these matters to them now. The prince, he said, seemed sad. "How shall we bring Siddhartha back to gaiety?" he asked.

The wise men answered, "Find the prince a bride!"

Reflecting among the thoughtless, awake among the
sleepers, the wise man advances like a racer
leaving behind the hack.

The Dhammapada (v. 29)

III

The Test of Manhood

*T*HIS BROODING, MEDITATIVE PRINCE – how will the king
arouse his active interest in women or marriage? The
maidens Siddhartha sees within the palace grounds are blushing,
shy girls who skitter away in excited confusion whenever the
handsome prince approaches; sometimes he hears their bell-like
chatter, like the excited chirping of birds, their titters and laughter
behind a garden wall. He himself is engaged in studies,
horsemanship, fencing, and archery; to such a young man, they
must have seemed foolish, flighty beings indeed.

Now being sixteen years of age, he would have seen and taken
pleasure in the temple dancers who on festive occasions per-
formed for the court. Abstractedly perhaps, he would have noted
their graceful movements and the deep beauty of their darkened
eyes, their long and shimmering black hair, and the gauze-like
delicacy of their clothes. Yet theirs were formal arts which may
well have interested him most for the artistry displayed. He knew
of course that some day he would marry and that his father would
make the necessary arrangements, even to selecting his bride, but
all that is likely to have seemed quite distant to a prince engaged in
what he regarded as more pressing, serious thoughts.

Again he pondered: why did the oxen need to move by means
of lashings? Why did the plough sever the worm? Why did the
peasant need to grunt and sweat to feed himself? Why did the bird
snatch up the seed, the insect, worms – only to be seized itself and

torn apart by predators? These seemed to him things to engage the serious attention of a man, not games with girls.

King Suddhodana read his son's heart right and wondered how nature's sure instinct, which draws together man and woman, might be fostered in the prince before it was too late and he had embarked on the religious life his father feared. Could it, indeed, be done?

The wise men seemed certain that it could. "What cannot be chained with iron bonds, O king," they said, "is oft held fast securely by a single strand of woman's hair."

Many ways might have to be tried, they argued, and it would be best to experiment to find the most efficacious lure.

"Most noble king," they said, "as we do not know what maiden in the land appeals to our prince, we urge you to summon the fairest daughters of all the noble families to a contest, wherein the graces and the beauty of each shall be judged by the prince himself. Let the maidens prepare themselves most fetchingly to win the finest prize, and let them come before the prince, each to receive a gift from him, and let us station ourselves close, to note how Prince Siddhartha greets each one. Perhaps we shall see him start and quicken at the sight of some girl he has not met before. Then we shall know with whom to bait our trap, to keep Siddhartha in the place of kings."

The plan seemed good to Suddhodana. Emissaries were sent across the length and breadth of his land, and to the lands of neighbouring kings as well, requesting that on such and such a day, they bring to Suddhodana's palace the fairest of their daughters, to receive a gift at the hands of the young prince, to honour their beauty.

No fewer than five hundred Sakyas are said to have prepared to send their daughters.

With what care the maidens must have made their preparations! New saris were readied for the great event, one more delicate than the next, of the finest Persian and Indian cloths. All the arts of the cosmetician, the hairdresser, and the perfumer must have been taxed to the utmost and, finally on the appointed day, each of the noble contestants must have seemed like a sparkling jewel within the Indian heavens.

With what grace they carried themselves as they approached the seated prince, he of the solemn face, sitting in his silks and jewels, his eyes quiet and perhaps even slightly bored. Accustomed since birth to walking barefoot, these girls had the majestic, slow, and slightly undulating walk we can still see in their descendants. Straight as statues they stood, yet moved with fluidity and grace, each motion quiet and controlled, catlike and light, a walk trained in the art of dance.

Tresses gleaming, their eyes wondrously coloured, the palms of their hands and feet hennaed red, a lacquered spot between their eyebrows, they approached the prince, their eyes shyly averted.

The wise men in the room, the ministers and sages, and the king himself, watched intently to see the prince's reaction, however subtle it might be. Perhaps a tenseness in the neck, a sudden glance of meaning which would last only a split-second, a tremor in the hands, would betray the emotion they sought to find.

Each girl was assured a valuable gift, but there was one prize which had been pointed out to the prince as the most valuable: this, he was told, was for the one he chose as the fairest of them all. Who would receive it would be his decision alone.

The first maiden approached the prince. So great was her embarrassment when she neared him that she blushed, cast her glance downwards, and did not even look up when Siddhartha gave her the prize. No sooner was it in her hand, than she fled in excited confusion.

But what had happened? The prince had given her – the very first contestant – the finest prize, a necklace of the purest pearls! Yet he had done this with hardly a glance at her, abstractedly, as though he gave it without care!

There was no doubt about it: Siddhartha seemed little interested in this game of beauty, in this frivolous contest of the fair, and seemed to wish not to be bothered with so trivial a matter as to which among the girls was loveliest. And so he gave to the first the very best of gifts.

Well, thought the wise men, the best gift may indeed have been given and Prince Siddhartha may indeed be bored; all the more reason to watch him intently, for if he now reacts to any one of the young maidens, one may assume he has been smitten more powerfully than was thought possible. It would take love alone to dislodge such complete indifference.

One after another the maidens came and in each case the reaction of the prince proved to be the same. Siddhartha remained bored, though courteous as ever; always he had a kind and gentle thing to say to the young women. He said it, though, as he might address a young sister, with gentleness and tenderness, but without the love the king was anxious to behold. As for the girls, no sooner did they see the handsome prince, no sooner did they hear his words of congratulation, than they withdrew in excited confusion, not one daring to look into his eyes – so deep, so dark, so full of mystery.

Then came the last. Those who watched immediately noticed what was different about her: she approached the prince purposefully and self-assured. Her head was erect and her eyes remained set on Siddhartha, her glance maidenly, yet unafraid.

Siddhartha watched her approaching him and a tenseness came into the air which the wise men noted. They could see that the young prince marvelled at the girl's beauty and the unrivalled dignity of her bearing; here was a womanliness which matched the wondrous manhood of the prince.

"What, gentle prince," the maiden is said to have asked Siddhartha, "have you no prize for me?" And she held out her hand to him.

By some error, all the prizes had been given out; someone had miscalculated the number needed.

Siddhartha smiled. "Indeed, the prizes are all gone, yet for the very fairest of the fair, there is a prize from me!" And Siddhartha slipped his emerald necklace from his neck and clasped it about the maiden's waist.

"Who are you, maiden?" the young prince asked.

"Yasodhara," she answered.

Their lips smiled at each other, but their eyes, joining in a glance of recognition, were serious, for each knew what their meeting signified.

It is said that, later in his life, Prince Siddhartha, then already the Enlightened One, the Buddha, spoke of Yasodhara.

"We both knew what this meeting meant, for she and I had recognised each other. We had been husband and wife together in the past, in countless lives over the millions of years, and in that moment, when our eyes met, I remembered all."

He remembered lives with her – aeons past – when he was a young hunter and the world was new and lives before that, when he lived his time on earth as a great tiger and she his mate.

> "Lo, as hid seed shoots after rainless years,
> So good and evil, pains and pleasures, hates
> And loves, and all dead deeds, come forth again
> Bearing bright flowers or dark, sweet fruit or sour.
> Thus I was he and she Yasodhara;
> And while the wheel of birth and death turns round,
> That which hath been must be between us two."[7]

Now all who watched the prince had seen what had occurred and inwardly rejoiced, afterwards coming to King Suddhodana and saying, "The trap is set; now let us wed the prince!"

As was the custom, the decision for a marriage to take place was made by the parents. Accordingly, King Suddhodana asked Yasodhara's father for his daughter's hand, that she might wed his son.

The disappointing answer soon came back.

"Already many Aryan nobles have sought her hand," her father wrote. "According to the custom, the girl goes to the manliest of men. Devadatta, the great archer, has sought her hand, as has Ardjuna, whom no man can match upon a mount, and Nanda, greatest of swordsmen. All have asked for Yasodhara as their wife; what can your contemplative prince do that would outdo these three in manliness?"

Siddhartha, hearing this dispatch, smiled confidently and reassured his doubting father.

"Do not fear," he said, "for I know the manly arts as well and, wanting Yasodhara for my wife, I shall not fail. Let us call a tournament, father, a week from now, no more, and summon to it Devadatta, Ardjuna, and Nanda too, and let us see who shall rightfully earn the honour of this maiden's hand."

The three contenders must have smiled as they were called. How easily they would best this gentle, meditative prince! Well they remembered riding and playing with him and how, in hunting, his arrow would often miss its mark, and how in riding, he would often fall behind.

They did not know Siddhartha contrived deliberately to miss the mark, happy to see the living creature spared; they did not know that he would halt his horse and rest it whenever he saw it panting hard, then charge the exhaustion to himself.

The tourney was a great event for the whole land and nobles, lords, and princes from all lands close by attended. Townspeople too came in great numbers, to watch the highborn contend to see whose hand was strongest, surest, and most worthy of that beauteous jewel, Yasodhara.

Into the field rode Devadatta, Ardjuna and Nanda, laughing and confident. Yasodhara and all her kin arrived, she being carried as a bride. What a sight that must have been: litters decorated to outsparkle the flowers of the fields; the painted oxen drawing the shining cart, the musicians accompanying the procession, festively playing.

On seeing Siddhartha's three challengers, Yasodhara's heart grew heavy. She knew their reputations in the warlike arts and, though confident in her prince, she nevertheless feared that somehow they might outdo him. In such a case, she would certainly be married to one of them and she dismayed, for although each was himself nobly born and handsome, she now knew where her heart rested.

Then a great shout arose and all eyes turned to see the Prince Siddhartha ride into the field atop his mighty white stallion

Kantaka. The horse, startled at the sight of so many onlookers, is said to have reared and pawed the air, then plunged back down to ground, until Siddhartha soothed him. The gaiety, the festive air, the hundreds watching the event, struck Prince Siddhartha too and, for a moment, the thoughtful prince found himself startled. But then his eyes met those of Yasodhara and his heart rejoiced.

Leaping from his snorting steed, he gaily shouted to his three rivals and to all who came to watch, "He is not worthy of this noble pearl, who is not worthiest; let my rivals prove if I have dared too much in seeking her!"

The test of archery began.

Contests like this become, in their telling, events of legendary magnitude. And so, it is said, great drums with leather drumskins were placed one and a half miles distant, at Nanda and Ardjuna's request, and both young men pierced their centres with their arrows, to the great delight of the crowd. Devadatta stepped up and with great show demanded that his drumskin be placed a hundred yards yet further off and, as the crowd gasped and Yasodhara's heart sank, he sent his arrow singing through its centre.

"Best that!" Devadatta taunted, turning to the prince, and Yasodhara let fall her golden sari over her eyes, to hide her sadness.

The Prince strode up to Devadatta and addressed him.

"Fair cousin, out of courtesy, lend me your bow and let me test, to see if I can handle it!"

Devadatta smiled and offered his great bow; he knew it took uncommonly great strength to bend it even slightly. Tied with the tendons of oxen, it was said to have been made of three lacquered sapling trunks, and strung with silver cord. Siddhartha, with his fingertips alone, drew the silver cord until to everyone's amazement, the bowtips touched and then the bow itself snapped right in two.

Siddhartha smiled. "Devadatta, this is a toy for children. How can I find a bow fit for a man?"

Then he was told of a bow which for years had lain within a temple, for no man could bend it. It was a bow used by an earlier, stronger race of Aryas, and had belonged to Siddhartha's grandfather, Simhahanu, an old and black bow encrusted with precious gems, its shaft as broad as a strong warrior's hand.

"Let it be brought!" Siddhartha commanded, his eyes on Yasodhara. "For he who will not stretch his strength to utmost limits is unworthy of this bride!"

The legend says they placed Siddhartha's drum six miles away, until the huge drumskin seemed a mere speck on the horizon. No one saw Siddhartha's arrow flash, so swiftly was it released, but miles around the old and the infirm who could not come to watch the tournament were startled at the twang reverberating through the air. Runners were sent to fetch the arrow and presently came back, amazement in their eyes.

"The arrow, noble lords," they said, "shot through both skins and travelled yet another six miles on – and where it plunged to earth, a spring has shot forth, sending up cold, refreshing waters!" And to this day, the Spring of the Arrow is marked and reverenced in India.

Then came the contest with the sabres.

Nanda cut through a tree trunk six fingers in diameter, with just one slash; Ardjuna went him one finger better, and Devadatta three.

Siddhartha strode up to his father, King Suddhodana, and, scorning the heavy sabres, asked for the dress sword he wore, a fragile thing of beauty meant for show and ceremony. He took this light, thin blade and, with it, cut at a double-trunk with such uncommon strength that he slashed right through both widths with one stroke only. Yet so fast was his move and so clean his cut that the two trees did not fall and Nanda laughed and danced, saying that the Prince Siddhartha failed – and had forfeited his bride. Then a light breeze, sent it is said by gods, brushed the two trunks and sent them crashing down.

The last test was of horsemanship and Prince Siddhartha, seated astride the broad back of Kantaka, easily won out over the other suitors. But jealous Devadatta grumbled.

"This means nothing. It does not show the measure of his horsemanship and is a tribute only to his horse. Who would not win, riding Kantaka?"

And so they fetched a giant stallion, unbroken and ferocious, which three grooms held with chains, and brought it to the field. Pitch-black, with eyes flashing red fire, sweating and rearing and kicking, the killer horse fought the grooms who tried to saddle it. With help, they finally slipped on at least a bit and reins, and the crowd gasped as the four suitors tried their skill and luck.

None of the first three could sit the mount for more than a few seconds. The third to try, Ardjuna, was the best, staying on the maddened stallion for twice around the field, until the horse finally turned its head and, seizing Ardjuna's foot in its teeth, hurled him to the ground. It reared above him and was ready to plunge downwards to trample him with its mighty hooves, when grooms attacked it and drove it back.

Seeing this, the crowd shouted, "Stop the tournament! Do not let Prince Siddhartha try! No one can master this black horse!"

But Siddhartha is said to have walked calmly to where the three grooms held the stallion back with chains, and put one hand over the horse's eyes, bidding the grooms let go their hold. With his other hand, he stroked the horse's sweating neck and flanks, and spoke some soothing words to it, which none could hear. Then, in a moment, he leaped upon the beast's great back and rode it round the field, using his knees only to guide it.

The onlookers, who had watched in anxious silence, now shouted out their joy: "Let the contest end, for none is better than Siddhartha! The prince has won his prize!"

And the maiden Gopa Yasodhara was brought before him in her bridal costume, walking proudly and erect, her dark eyes shining now with happiness and love for her noble prince. She placed a wreath of flowers about his neck and rested her head upon his chest, saying, "Dear Prince, behold me, who am thine!"

The wedding date was set by the astrologers and great festivities were decreed for all. King Suddhodana completed for them the three palaces earlier described, one for each season, and after the wedding ceremonies, they went to begin their life together.[8] Still the king feared and did not trust love's bonds entirely, and had three rings of great walls built round about their palaces, guards set, and orders given that none should pass without the king's own seal, not even the royal prince.

Better than sovereignty over the earth, better than going
to heaven, better than Lordship over all words, is
the reward of the first step in holiness.

The Dhammapada (v. 178)

IV

The Great Renunciation

WITHIN THEIR JEWELLED AND GLITTERING prison did they
live their years and, presently, were blessed with a son, to
the great joy of King Suddhodana, who saw his line increased.

But Siddhartha was strangely troubled, though pleased enough
with the birth of his son.

"Does it not seem," he said, "as though an impediment has
been born, as though a fetter has been born?"

The king, troubled by his son's remark, thought to make light
of it, to treat it as a joke. And so Suddhodana named his infant
grandson Rahula, meaning "bond", "tie" or "impediment".

Deep within Siddhartha there stirred a growing discontent.
This despite the fact that his life was luxurious, that he was much
in love and happy with Yasodhara, despite the languid evenings
filled with music and dancing and laughter – despite the fact that
nothing was left undone which might add pleasure to his years. As
for signs of human suffering or even of the transience of human
life, these were walled out by the king's edict.

Often the prince rode alone, slowly and thoughtfully, through
the grounds of his palaces, astride Kantaka; often, too, he rode in
his chariot, with only his close attendant, the charioteer Channa,
beside him. Silent these two rode, the prince lost in an unease too
vague yet to be defined, as though a voice deep within him called
in a language he did not yet understand.

Then came the Four Encounters which changed all.

One day, after the birth of Rahula, Siddhartha bade Channa ready the chariot again. After years within the palace walls, he had obtained his father's consent to venture out again. King Suddhodana reasoned that, despite all other considerations, Siddhartha must be permitted to see the life of those he was to govern. Already, the prince was in his late twenties, and had need to know of life.

Yet not too much did the king wish him to see. Again, heralds were sent ahead of the prince, ordering the infirm and old to stay indoors, and forbidding all funerals. The streets once more were watered and swept, the houses gaily decorated, and the populace dressed as for a holiday.

Into the sundrenched town rode Siddhartha and Channa and all rejoiced.*

"How fair the world is after all," Siddhartha said, smiling at his charioteer, "when all these good people need to make them happy is to see their prince!"

Yet, suddenly, out of one of the houses on the road, stumbled a wretched, ancient man, full of the infirmities of his many years. His shrivelled body, on which the skin hung like loose, wrinkled parchment, was covered with foul and tattered rags; his eyes were full of pus and virtually unseeing; his jaws were empty of their teeth and trembled weakly; his matted hair had thinned and hung in patches; his withered left arm hung beside him, flapping like a rag, while with the other he leaned upon a staff, to support his shaking body as it inched along the street.

"Alms!" the wretch cried and his ribs heaved and gasped at each weak breath. "Alms! Good people, help! For the love of the gods, help me, for I am near to death!"

Siddhartha bade Channa stop and watched in amazement. The frightened people in the street, however, seeing that the apparition had defied the king's command to stay away, surrounded the old man and hurried him indoors.

* According to some accounts, the four encounters Siddhartha was now to make were within the palace gardens, one at each of its compass-points.

But they were too late, for Siddhartha had seen – and had been shaken. He turned to Channa.

> "Channa, what thing is this who seems a man,
> Yet surely only seems, being so bowed,
> So miserable, so horrible, so sad?
> Are men born sometimes thus? What meaneth he
> Moaning, 'Tomorrow or next day I die?'
> Finds he no food so that his bones jut forth?
> What woe has happened to this piteous one?"[9]

Of course Siddhartha would have seen old men around the palace of his father, but those appeared quite different. They were all healthy, nobly dressed, well-groomed, dignified; they did not resemble in the least this ailing wretch, in the last extremities of decrepitude. What Siddhartha encountered in the street, then, was not merely old age, but a miserable, suffering old age, the kind he had never been permitted to see.

Channa, though frightened to give answer, replied out of love for Siddhartha.

"This is nothing else but an old man, dear prince! Some sixty years ago, his back was straight, his eyes were bright; he played at games, sang, loved, sported, and laughed. Then with the years, infirmities set in, and Time, that great defiler, sucked the vital strength from him, until today you see him wizened and weak, a mockery of manhood, through no fault of his."

"But can this happen to others as well," Siddhartha asked, "or is this his alone?"

"To all it happens," Channa said.

"Even to Yasodhara and me?" the prince asked.

"Even so, my Lord!"

Siddhartha turned to his charioteer and said, "Take me home, Channa, and let me ponder this, for I have seen something today which I did not expect to see."

Hearing what had happened, Suddhodana had the watch doubled on the gates, but it was only a matter of days before the prince again entreated him to let him venture out once more. This time he told his father that he knew the way had been prepared especially for him, to spare him anguish.

"I am grateful, Lord, for your loving concern to spare me pain," Siddhartha said, "but I now wish to walk about dressed as an ordinary man whom none could recognise, to see life in the town as it is really lived."

"Perhaps," the king said to his ministers after the prince had left, "this second visit will repair the damage of the first. We all know how the hunting falcon startles at whatever he sees, when first his hood has been removed, yet how he looks at things with confidence and strength, once they have become familiar to his glance. A quiet eye comes of freedom, so let my son see all; just let me know of his reactions!"

The next morning, the gates opened to two men, a merchant and a clerk by dress, who carried the king's seal. They were the prince and his charioteer, going on foot unrecognised even by the guards who checked their passes. Setting his feet towards the town, Siddhartha spoke to his companion of what the two of them had seen that other, fateful, time.

"If all beauty fades, Channa, how can one take delight in beauty? Such delight, such grasping, is foolishness, Channa; it is like trying to hold the water of the brook, or seize the wind. How strange that men run after and attempt to seize that which inevitably passes! How strange they fail to see the wizened skin and sightless eyes behind the rosy lips and young complexion!" Channa deferentially kept silent, though he was troubled at the prince's words.

Into the town they came and wandered about, seeing all sights: the merchants selling fruits and vegetables; the oxen wandering the streets; the armourer hammering to shape his swords and helmets; the children sitting cross-legged before their guru, reciting the names of gods. Here a young bride entered a temple to pray for the birth of a son, and there a proud Brahman stepped, dis-

daining the lowly; the rich passed by, carried in painted palan-
quins, not recognising the prince they knew, dressed now in
merchant's clothes. Everywhere about them bustled life, activity,
laughter, and much talk – dramatic contrast to the quiet palace
gardens. Siddhartha took great pleasure in the colourful display.

Suddenly he stopped.

There was a different voice now in the air, above the hum and
bustle of the street, a sound strange to his ears, and dolorous. He
looked about him to find out whence it came and then his eyes
noted beside the road, lying in the dust in front of a house, a poor
and infirm man trying to get up.

"Help me, masters, help! Help, or I die before I can return to
my own home!" he cried, gasping for air.

His body quivered and was seized with spasms which
convulsed his frame; his skin was covered with unsightly blotches
and his head was bathed in sweat; pain twisted his mouth and
caused his eyes to roll about in their sockets in a delirium of fever.
He dragged himself along the earth, clutching the dust, and
hauled himself half up, only to fall back down to earth again, lying
there trembling and exhausted.

Siddhartha ran to him and took his head upon his lap, soothing
the ailing man with tender hands.

"Brother, what has befallen thee?" Siddhartha asked. "What is
amiss?"

Then, turning to Channa who stood beside him in an agony of
spirit, Siddhartha asked, "Why is it that this man cannot arise?
Why does he gasp for breath and shake and tremble so? Why
burns his skin and why is it deformed with spots the like of which
I never saw?"

Channa felt a great pain go through his heart, but he answered
nevertheless.

"Great prince," Channa replied, "this man is seized by plague
or pestilence, is eaten up inside by fevers, until his body houses
corruption only. The blood boils in him, the heart almost gives
out, the lungs cannot suck the healthful air, and his legs are like
water on which he cannot stand. Within his frame lives agony

alone and his eyes are delirious with the ailment which has taken possession of him. Come, prince, it is not good to hold him close like that, for the disease he has may leap even to you!"

But Siddhartha would not leave the stricken man, and continued comforting him. Under the prince's compassionate touch, the sick man's convulsions slowed. His eyes closed softly as in the balm of sleep, the breath became less laboured, and there grew a quiet in the man he had not known for days.

"Channa," said the prince, looking up at his attendant, "is this, then, a thing which may befall anyone? Are there others like him on this earth?"

"Indeed there are, great prince!" Channa replied. "All mankind is subject to the thing we call disease, even as this man is."

"Do such things come unobserved and unsuspected?"

"They do," Channa replied. "Like the snake which strikes unseen, biting the sleeper, or the tiger who leaps from the jungle onto the traveller upon the path, disease comes suddenly, as chance may send it, and there is nothing one may do to halt its flight over the earth."

"Then that must mean, dear Channa," Siddhartha said, "that all men live in fear, that none can say with certainty, going to sleep at night, that he shall rise up strong again the next morning."

"Even so, my prince!" Channa replied.

"And what comes after illness, Channa? Is it a broken body, like this wretch – and then old age such as we saw the other day?"

"Yes, my Lord, that is so, for those who live so long!"

"Live so long? What do you mean, Channa?" Siddhartha asked.

"I mean, sweet prince, that there are those who may not wish to bear their agonies and also those whose bodies will not last until old age, like broken chariots which cannot end the journey."

"What happens then?" Siddhartha asked.

"They die."

And at that moment, Channa turned and pointed riverward. Siddhartha looked and saw a wailing, sobbing procession and, carried by it, a litter on which lay a corpse.

"That is a dead man, prince!" the charioteer said.

Sprinkled with red and yellow dust, the dead man lay stiff, while all about him his kinfolk cried, "Rama! Rama!" – the god invoked at times of death.

Siddhartha followed, having seen to it that the ailing man was carried home by friends. The prince now watched as mourners placed the corpse on top of the timbers which would soon consume it in flames. He felt like an empty vessel now, drained of all his princely thoughts, and receiving powerful new impressions, which had momentous impact upon his heart and mind.

"See the flames consume the bodily shell, O prince!" said Channa. "That is the fate of all men and women. When the flames have died, nothing but ashes and a few bits of white bone remain and even the birds will not find anything of value on that mound. See him, Lord – a short while back he was like other men, enjoying life in company of friends and relatives; taking delight in children, music, and the dance; seeking out pleasure, now here, now there; working for his bread, and finding life full. Then some chance accident perhaps – a tile from off a roof, a poisonous snake, a foul breeze, some tainted water – and he is no more!"

"Such, then, is life?" Siddhartha asked.

"It is, even so, my lord!" Channa agreed.

"Come, Channa, let us leave this place, and let me muse on what I have seen today."

The prince's heart was heavy. Many a day did he puzzle over the sights he had seen; many a night the fair Yasodhara had saddened at his troubled look. It seemed he took no more delight in her or in their son.

"Find you no haven in me, my lord?" she asked, stroking his head one night.

"Yes, my sweet bride, but the haven I find in your arms is but a brief respite on my journey. It is like a beautiful town through which a traveller passes, never to see it again. And so it is bittersweet. How can we find true and lasting delight, when life's impermanence, its decay, stares at us through the face of old age, sickness, and death? All this about us," and Siddhartha gestured towards the rich ornaments and furnishings within the room, "all this shall be swept away by Time: the trees and gardens shall die, the palaces crumble into dust, and even you and I, despite our young love now, will watch each other sink, as Time claims all our strength. Rahula, here beside you, finds himself born – and birth means life, and life means death. In birth is the very cause of all that follows; death is the very child of birth and pain – the price of life."

So did Prince Siddhartha begin to reason about such things.

On a certain day, Channa had orders to prepare the chariot again and once more the two of them set forth, to view the world and meet the sights the gods, they say, had sent Siddhartha's way, as calls with which to waken him from the deep sleep of luxury and delights. This time, rattling down a dusty road, they saw a figure underneath a tree.

"Slow down, Channa," the prince ordered, "and let me see what manner of man this is."

Under the tree beside the edge of the road, seated cross-legged as the gurus did, was a man whose face struck Prince Siddhartha as powerfully, yet differently, as had the sight of the three others he had seen.

"What sort of man is this?" Siddhartha asked. "He is poor, for only rags cover him, and he is old and thin, like the other aged man we came across, yet there is no pain, no suffering in this face! He is at peace, serene, and radiates great love and kindness, and what seems to me great understanding. There is joy in that face as well, Channa! Who is he?"

"He, noble lord, is a *rishi* of the forest, a homeless monk and wanderer in search of truth, a man who has renounced the worldly life. His eyes are cleared by worship of the gods and by great disciplines. No longer is he beset by *Maya*, by illusion; having left all, he has found all. That is why such men as he have found abiding peace."

Siddhartha marvelled and turned home and again pondered deeply what he had just seen.

It came to him that he must find an answer to the riddle of human life and a cure for human suffering. Somewhere that answer and that cure were to be found – of this Siddhartha felt certain – and find it he must! For his heart increasingly felt compassion for mankind and, for him, to feel compassion meant to act.

Yasodhara was not kept ignorant of the state of her husband's heart and mind, nor of the answering decision that was being called forth from him.

"What good are all the prayers, wife, which our priests offer unto the gods?" Siddhartha asked. "None at all, it seems to me, for either the gods are powerless to stop the pain and suffering of man, or they are evil. If powerless, why pray to them, why seek their intercession? Why offer sacrifices? If they are evil, then it is clear that all the more we must find ways for man to stand alone, for him to find an answer helpful to himself." So reasoned Prince Siddhartha.

And it seemed to the young prince, now twenty-nine years old, that it was he himself who must find the answer for mankind. What stirred in him was the longing and yearnings of millennia, of countless lives, in which, the legends say, he had perfected himself to that point where he might in this life achieve Buddhahood.

How to go about his task? Siddhartha recalled the happy, peaceful, and serene ascetic whom he had seen by the roadside. It seemed to him that this man pointed the way towards enlightenment, to the supreme knowledge. It lay, Siddhartha reasoned, in cutting all fetters with the perfumed past and in going off alone to seek the answers, through hardship and, if need be, pain, in reducing one's life to such slight requirements that the entire being might be concerned only with the most final of all questions.

And a voice in him murmured, "The time is now ... the time is now!"

One day, while walking pensively through the palace gardens, pondering his changing fate, Siddhartha heard the sweet voice of a Kshatriya maid, Kisa Gotami, singing softly to herself. He looked up and saw the girl gazing at him with eyes of love and he heard her voice singing:

> "Happy indeed is the Mother,
> Happy indeed is the Father,
> Happy indeed is the Wife,
> Who has such a Husband!"

This young woman, like so many others, had become entranced with him. The accounts all speak of his beauty; we are told he was stately, tall, well-formed; that his skin, the colour of pure gold, was without blemish; that his muscles were as a lion's; that his eyes were clear as a hawk's, yet warm and gentle; that his stride and stance were noble and dignified. It is said that there was about him even in those days a radiance, and his approach was said to have gladdened the hearts of men and stirred the hearts of maidens.

"Well spoken," Siddhartha thought of the maiden's song. "But what is it that must be done if eternal happiness is to be achieved? The happiness of which this girl sings may pass; it is here one moment and gone the next. How, then, is eternal happiness, a happiness which does not change, dissolve, or die, to be won?"

A thought came to him that what must be done is this: wrong understanding and cravings of all kinds must be extinguished, the fires of craving must be quenched, and in this snuffing out of flames which devour a man's inner being lay an end to suffering and, thus, lasting happiness.

"The maiden has taught me a good lesson," the prince thought. "Certainly, it is Nirvana – perfect bliss – that I am looking for. It behoves me this very day to quit the household life and to retire from the world in search of it. I shall send this lady a teacher's fee!" And as a sign of how valuable he thought her lesson to be, Siddhartha loosened from his neck a pearl necklace worth a hundred thousand pieces of money and sent it to Kisa Gotami. She thought the gift signified that the prince loved her, and rejoiced; he, however, went to his chamber and lay upon his bed. He determined to leave, but not without his father's consent.

The king, however, responded only by increasing the guards at his gates and along the roads, and by ordering the palace dancing girls to tempt and lure the prince to stay.

But it was too late already for such temptations. For many days and nights, the palace thrilled to song and laughter, lights were never permitted to be dimmed, and dancing never stopped. Wherever the young prince walked, he was confronted by beautiful maidens, luring him – all in vain.

Then came the fateful night which Buddhist scriptures call the Great Renunciation. Siddhartha lay on his couch and awakened to look about him. There, lying about on pillows and couches everywhere in the room were dancing girls exhausted by their merry-making, asleep in languid and licentious poses. As Siddhartha looked at them with sadness and even with disgust, it suddenly seemed to him as though they were all transformed into grotesque old hags. The dresses they wore now seemed mildewed and torn, were falling apart from age, and their now-toothless gums offered hideous grins through shrivelled lips. That vision, it is said, was sent as a reminder by the gods, for Siddhartha to hesitate no longer, a sign again that all created things must age and die, and that truth alone remains eternal.

Siddhartha left the room and called to Channa. "Ready my horse Kantaka; I ride forth tonight and you shall come with me upon its back!"

While Channa saddled the white steed, Siddhartha opened the door to the bedroom of his wife and son. Yasodhara lay on a couch strewn deep with jasmine and other blossoms; her hand lay on the head of the sleeping child beside her. The room gave off the sweet fragrance of the flowers and of the aromatic oils feeding a bedside lamp. Siddhartha stepped inside and stood within the doorway. Silently, he said farewell.

"I long to take you in my arms, Yasodhara, and kiss you and Rahula goodbye. Yet I know that, if I did so, you might awaken and, that if you did, I might not leave. When I have become a Buddha I shall return to see my son."

Kantaka stamped his hooves in the moonlight as the prince approached. Siddhartha took one last look around, then leaped onto the saddle, as nimbly as he had mounted years ago to win his bride by taming a black charger. Now there were other beasts to tame – within himself, another contest in which to try his strength, and a great prize to win, the one he thought the noblest of them all.

Channa leaped on behind and Kantaka started for the palace walls. The legend has it that there, miraculously, the gates stood open and the guards all slept, for the gods made certain that none could impede the coming Buddhahood. A hush lay over everything, as though the earth's breath was bated.

At the moment Siddhartha prepared to pass through the open gate, Mara, the tempter, is said to have appeared before him in the skies, urging him not to depart. In this "first temptation", Mara promised him dominion over "the four great islands and the two hundred small islands that surround them".[10] But Prince Siddhartha, now truly a Bodhisattva – one who aspires to Buddhahood – refused the promise of earthly dominion, whereupon Mara, thwarted this time, promised to follow his path, watching for new opportunities to tempt. "Henceforth," he said, "whenever thou hast a thought of lust or malice or cruelty, I shall know."[11]

Through the gates sped the prince, then galloped down the lanes until, near dawn, he reached the banks of the River Anoma, at the kingdom's frontier, where Siddhartha stopped. Nearby, sat a beggar.

As Channa watched wide-eyed, Siddhartha exchanged his rich and royal clothing with the mendicant, putting on the beggar's worn green and rust-coloured rags, the hues of forest leaves, which he would wear henceforth. Then, with his sword, he cut off his long hair, a mark of his nobility, and gave his jewels and sword to Channa.

"Take these and my horse Kantaka, faithful Channa, and return them to the king, my father, and tell him what I have done – what I must do!"

And, as the tearful Channa mounted the steed and, under protest, turned Kantaka back to the palace, he glanced once more over his shoulder, at his beloved prince.

It is said that he saw his prince striding to the water's edge like a great conqueror, with joy and resolution in his step, knowing himself now to be no longer Prince Siddhartha, but Gautama the beggar, seeking Truth.

A Dhyani Buddha. Terrace of Borobodur Stupa, Java.
8th Century CE.

Let us live happily, then, though we call nothing our
own! We shall be like the bright gods, feeding on
happiness!

The Dhammapada (v. 200)

V

The Great Inner Struggle

*F*OR SEVEN DAYS, THE FUTURE Buddha sat in contemplation in
a nearby mango grove called Anupiya, filled with joy at having
retired from the world. Then he arose, and, gathering together the
eight requisites of a devotee which henceforth would be the limits
of his possessions – three robes, an alms bowl, a razor, a needle, a
belt, and a water-strainer – he strode to Rajagaha, a town about
ninety miles away.

There, for the first time in his life, he begged his food, holding
out his bowl from door to door. But he had not been in the town
for long before news of his arrival reached the ears of the local
ruler, a pious king named Bimbisara.

"My lord," the king's messengers had announced, "there is a
being of remarkable appearance within our town, begging food.
He does not look like an ordinary rishi, but like a great and noble
lord; we do not know whether he is a divine spirit, a man, or a
demon!"

Bimbisara told his men to keep watch carefully. "If he is a man,"
the king said, "he will consume that which he has begged; if he is
non-human, he will vanish once he leaves the city." And so the
future Buddha was carefully observed throughout his visit to the
town.

Having collected a few scraps of food, enough to still the imme-
diate call of hunger, Gautama left and sat down on a rock outside

the town, preparing to eat. But no sooner had his princely palate encountered these scraps from humble tables than a feeling of terrible nausea overcame him and he was filled with disgust. This was food the like of which he had never eaten! His taste had been trained in palace delicacies and sweets; he found himself almost retching as he now faced the miserable fare in his humble begging bowl.

Then he began to admonish himself, saying, "Siddhartha, even though you were raised in a family where only the best food was offered you, even though you lived in luxury and ease, the moment you saw a monk dressed in discarded rags you said to yourself, 'Oh, if I could only be like him, be dressed like him, and eat like him!' But now that you have your wish and have renounced all, what, pray, are you doing?"

And, having thus reprimanded himself, he found that his nausea disappeared, and he ate his food gratefully.

The king's men, who had observed this, hastened back to Bimbisara to tell him what had transpired. King Bimbisara was anxious to meet this holy man who by his radiance and noble air had caused so great a commotion in his town, and so he went outside the gates and approached the future Buddha. Taking pleasure in Gautama's modest deportment, Bimbisara addressed him and asked, "Who are you and what do you seek?"

"Great king," the future Buddha said, "for me there is no delight in wealth or in the pleasures of the senses, for they defile. I have retired from the world, seeking complete enlightenment!"

Bimbisara looked at the young man in amazement and with pleasure. "Truly," he said, "you shall become a Buddha! I ask only this, that when you do, you shall first visit my kingdom." Gautama recognised Bimbisara's pious intent and agreed. Then he set his feet again on his path.

He had heard of the Brahmanic sage Alara Kalapa, and wishing for a guru, a teacher who might guide him towards enlightenment, he travelled to see this ascetic philosopher.

Here is what the Buddha himself later on told his disciples about this period of his life:

"And having thus retired from the world and craving the *summum bonum*, the incomparable peaceful state, I drew near to where Alara Kalapa was; and having drawn near, I spoke to Alara Kalapa as follows:

" 'Brother Kalapa, I would like to lead the religious life under your guidance and discipline.' "

The guru welcomed Gautama. "Such is this doctrine," he said of his teaching, "that in no long time an intelligent man can learn for himself, realise, and live in the possession of all that his master has to teach."

And, indeed, it did not take the future Buddha long to learn this teaching. Once he had mastered it, he approached his teacher and asked him how far this teaching went, how far it took a man along the spiritual paths. Alara Kalapa told him it took a disciple "to that realm which is devoid of materiality."

Then the future Buddha, the searcher Gautama, thought to himself that he was not inferior to Alara Kalapa; that he, like his guru, possessed the faith, heroism, contemplation, concentration, and wisdom of which his teacher spoke. And it was clear to Gautama that he would soon be able to reach the realm devoid of materiality.

Quickly he achieved that stage of meditation and, having dwelt therein, he came again to Alara Kalapa and announced the fact. His teacher must have immediately recognised the truth of the future Buddha's assertion, for he rejoiced and asked Gautama to help him in leading his followers.

"Thus, O priests," the Buddha said later, "did Alara Kalapa, my teacher, take me, his pupil, and make me every whit the equal of himself, and honour me with very great honour. And it occurred to me, O priests, as follows:

"This doctrine does not lead to aversion, absence of passion, cessation, quiescence, knowledge, supreme wisdom, and Nirvana, but only as far as this realm.

"And I, O priests, did not honour that doctrine with my adhesion, and being averse to that doctrine, I departed on my journey."

Still craving the *summum bonum*, the incomparable peaceful state, as he called it, the future Buddha travelled to the place where lived Uddaka Ramaputta, a Brahmanic master, with his seven hundred disciples. He asked this famed teacher (very likely of Upanishadic ideas) whether he might live among his disciples and study his teaching. Again, the future Buddha had the same experience: again he comprehended the teaching very quickly, and to its very limits. These Uddaka announced as the "realm of neither perception nor yet non-perception", neither conscious nor unconscious.

Uddaka, soon recognising Gautama's religious gifts, offered him the leadership of his school, but he declined. "This doctrine," he said, "does not lead to aversion, absence of passion, cessation, quiescence, knowledge, supreme wisdom, and Nirvana..." Once again, having spent less than a year with these two teachers, the future Buddha turned his quest elsewhere. Five fellow disciples of Uddaka left with him; these five, who came to be called "those of the happy group", became Gautama's close companions and, ultimately, the first to hear him expound his own teaching.

What is this Nirvana which the Buddha sought? And how might it be described?

Nirvana is! says the Buddhist, for he knows that only he who has experienced it can know its nature. And even he cannot convey it to others, for the truth which can be expressed in words is not the real truth. It implies the highest state of consciousness possible, far above that experienced by human beings ordinarily, yet inhabiting all potentially, awaiting their response to its inner call. Buddhists define Nirvana as "the inner state which the Enlightened attain".

The Buddha himself never defined Nirvana, having attained to it, for it was his mission to bring people to it, not to explain it. He knew that it needs to be reached to be understood; yet, from the hints he gave, we understand that in this vast expansion of consciousness is to be found "the end of woe".

It is really not so strange that we cannot define Nirvana. There are other realities we cannot describe. We cannot, for example, tell another person what a flower smells like, what an apple tastes like. or what a piece of music sounds like. No words exist; each must make these discoveries for himself. Indeed, words are not only inadequate, they are positively misleading, being subjective, and implying one thing for one and something else for another. Words are abstractions; Nirvana, says the Buddhist, is the end of illusion – "Reality seen face to face".[12]

Still seeking his Buddhahood, his enlightenment, Gautama walked to Uruvela, in the country of the Magadhans. In his own words:

"There I perceived a delightful spot with an enchanting grove of trees, and a silvery flowing river, easy of approach and delightful, and a village nearby in which to beg... Truly, there is everything here necessary for a youth of good family who is desirous of struggling.

"And then I settled down, as everything was suitable for struggling."

The future Buddha had decided that he had gone as far as he could with the aid of teachers; the rest of the Way he would have to serve as his own guide. Here he was joined by his companions, the five ascetics, the chief among whom was named Kondanna. He was the youngest of eight astrologers and fortune-tellers whom King Suddhodana had consulted when Prince Siddhartha was born; the other four were the sons of four of the seven other counsellors.

Now Gautama entered upon his most severe efforts. He reduced his food intake to the point where, it is said, he lived on single grains of rice; utterly oblivious of the harshness of his life, he undeviatingly pursued his goal. He sat cross-legged, in what is called the "lotus" position*, and fasted in the extreme.

For six full years, Gautama existed in this way, subjected to the blazing heat of the day and the icy coldness of the winter nights; the snow, hail and rain pelted him unmercifully and the wind howled against his still and shrivelled form. Back erect, hands folded in his lap, Gautama sat, his golden skin turning dark and leathery from exposure, his lips cracked, his almost-shut eyes mere sparks in deep caverns, his ribs jutting forth.

"The bones of my spine," he was to say later, "when bent and straightened, were like a row of spindles... And as a bitter gourd cut off raw, is cracked and withered by the sun, so was my skin withered from lack of food."

The five disciples continued with him through these years, impressed by the extremities of asceticism to which Gautama subjected himself, watching and waiting, trusting that these frightful austerities would bring him to Buddhahood.

"My body reached a state of extreme emaciation," Gautama was later quoted as saying. "My limbs became like the dry and knotted joints of bamboo. My buttocks became like a buffalo's hoof, and my spine with its protruding vertebrae became like beads on a string. My ribs were visible like the exposed rafters of a dilapidated house. Just as in a deep well the surface of the water gleams far below, so my pupils, sunk deep in their sockets, gleamed far below. Just as a bitter gourd, when it is cut, quickly dries up and shrivels in the sun, so my scalp dried up and shrivelled. If I wanted to touch my belly-skin, I encountered my backbone, because the

---

* The cross-legged "lotus" posture, one of several basic "yogic positions", is not merely traditional, but also practical. Some claim that, by reducing the flow of blood to the lower extremities, it feeds the brain; it is also seen by yogis as making them virtually immovable, for it anchors the person adopting it to the ground, in such a way that, even if they should faint, they would not topple over and risk injury. Not only does it keep the joints flexible, but keeps the spine erect – essential to good breathing. Called by some the "Hero posture", it provides a feeling of calm in which it is possible to focus and concentrate one's attention. A French Benedictine monk calls it in his book, *Christian Yoga*, "an attitude of recollectedness".

two had come so close together. If I wanted to pass excrement or urine, I fell over on my face. If I rubbed my limbs, the hair, rotted at the roots, came away in my hand."[13]

One day, at the end of six years of such efforts, he bathed in the river Nairanjana, but found himself too weak to emerge from the waters. Finally, he dragged himself to the bank of the river by holding onto a tree branch, but then staggered and fell, unable to move. He might have died, had not a herdsman's daughter, Sujata by name, passed by chance and, seeing his state, restored his strength with a drink of rice-milk.

He realised then that this asceticism, like the philosophy of Alara Kalapa and Uddaka, could not lead him towards the fulfilment of his aim. Not only were all these ways useless, they were also dangerous. The philosophy of the two Brahmin teachers could lead to complacency, while the extreme asceticism of the mountain rishis could lead to a destruction of the faculties. Gautama had subjected himself to the extremes of asceticism in order to silence the bodily appetites, to still the calls the body makes upon the consciousness, to bring the physical organism under stern control. But starvation, he found, did not bring enlightenment; to achieve so mighty a goal, his organism would have to be healthy to the full. This Gautama understood, now on the riverbank.

It seemed to him also that all the ways he had tried were essentially self-centred. Both of the Brahmins whom he had first followed taught a doctrine aimed at bringing the individual to a state of inner power, of self-mastery, which might make him virtually superhuman. Great was this goal, the future Buddha admitted, but it was not his own; it was too limited, for it offered no solution to the problem of human suffering. Gautama rejected any teaching which seemed to lack in compassion and which did not try to solve the problem of human existence for all.

Asceticism, he concluded, was a way that was as self-centred as those taught by his two Brahmin teachers. Who would benefit from the excessive disciplines to which he had subjected himself for the past years? Certainly not others. Perhaps he, Gautama, might actually achieve tremendous powers over his body, be liberated from serfdom to its appetites, but where would that lead, if not to death? He had seen the many holy men and ascetics in the mountains, undergo terrible privations, abusing and even torturing themselves. Who, except they, could possibly benefit? For whom were they following their practices? Only for themselves, for their own psychic powers, for a personal perfection which would enable them to draw nearer to the gods. And Gautama doubted the very existence of gods and souls. Of only one thing was this future Buddha now certain: if life is suffering, there must be a cause of suffering, there must be an end to suffering, and there must be a way towards achieving a cessation of suffering. He was determined to find the truth concerning these questions and, when he found it, offer it to suffering mankind, not merely use it for himself.

The future Buddha took his seat once again and began meditating. But now, restored as he was by nourishment, he was seen – and rejected – by the five disciples who had followed him. Gautama, they concluded, had abandoned asceticism, had given up.

"He was not even able by the austerity of six years to achieve Buddhahood," they said to each other. "How is it possible for him to do so now that he accepts ordinary food? He is defeated in the effort; for us to look for benefit from him is as if one should think of trying to wash one's head in a dewdrop!" And, taking their robes and begging bowls, they left the future Buddha and went to Rishipatana, one hundred and forty miles away, near Benares.

Gautama, alone now, gradually repaired his emaciated body. He began to accept the food-offerings which villagers from the surrounding countryside had been placing beside him for some time – and which he had in the past hardly touched, leaving all but a few grains of rice for the birds and animals to have. Also, he began venturing forth again, to beg his one meal a day in the towns. Now that he understood what unchecked asceticism led to, his compassion for mankind prompted him one day to approach one haggard self-torturer whom he met on the road.

"Much-suffering sir!" the future Buddha said to the ascetic, whom he recognised as one to whom others had shown deference. "I, like you, am a seeker after truth, and I see round about me brothers who are anguished and tortured. Why would you wish to add misery to a life already filled with woe?"

"It is said," replied the ascetic, "that if a man endures such pain in life that death would seem voluptuous rest, he will gain great merit, having cleansed his soul of sin and freed it to live in splendour through all eternity."

"But, look," Gautama said, "look at the sky. There floats a cloud which once was ocean spray or river water and which is destined to return to earth again as rain, then rise again as mist, as cloud, then fall again, in endless repetition. Perhaps this is the way with man as well. If it is, then all the tortures you undergo today will be repeated yet again and again, for evermore. Then the rest you seek will never come."

The ascetic grew annoyed. Who was this stranger, so young in years, who dared to challenge what the wise men taught? Sharply, he rebuked Gautama.

"See here!" he said. "This much we know: the body clogs our soul; the bodily shell holds down that which seeks to rise, it fetters the spirit. And so we torture it, until we are free of it, masters of it, oblivious to it. It is a great gamble, a game of dice we play with the gods, but the stakes are high enough to make the game worthwhile!"

Gautama looked at the old man compassionately. How could he get the man to understand? Indeed, even he was not yet sure of anything, did not yet have that perfected understanding which would be his upon enlightenment. Still, even now he was convinced this ascetic's words did not make sense to an intelligent man.

"Supposing, holy sir," Gautama said, "that you are right and you shall win rest, for even a million years. Still, even that must end sometime, for all things seem to me to change, nothing in all the worlds seems permanent. Tell me, do your gods live on forever? Speak!"

"They do not," the ascetic replied. "Only Brahma endures; the gods merely live."

"This being so," Gautama said, "why gamble with your dice, which are your moans and groans, to chance after something which may only be a dream or, being not a dream, will surely end? Why destroy this body, maim it, punish it, even mutilate it, when it is your chariot, meant to carry you in your quest?"

Now the old ascetic was extremely vexed. "Look here!" he said, brushing Gautama aside, "This is our road and we shall walk it even if all its stones are turned to flame! Speak up, if you know a better way! If not, leave us alone."

What a challenge that must have seemed to the compassionate Gautama! How his heart must have yearned to tell the old man a better way, a kinder way, a loftier way! But, in truth, he did not know that way as yet, and he walked away with pity in his heart and tears in his eyes.

As he was passing along the road, he encountered a large flock of sheep and goats being driven by a shepherd. At the end, he noted one lamb which had hurt its leg and was limping. He picked it up and held it to his breast, and then it came to him that it was far, far better for a man to comfort even one small animal than to sit and watch the sorrows of the world, passively among the praying priests.

Perhaps he did not yet fully appreciate it, but in this thought was established a different direction from the Brahmanism all about him and in which he was reared. The future Buddha now realised even more clearly the need for a compassionate, loving, and altruistic teaching, and he was turning evermore from the rituals and prayers which characterised the faith of his fathers.

"Friend herdsman!" he called out. "Where are you bringing these sheep and goats at noon, seeing that they are customarily folded at dark?"

"We have been sent," the man replied, "to fetch a hundred sheep and a hundred goats for our king, so that he may this evening make them into blood-sacrifices to the gods."

"I shall come with you!" Gautama said, and took his place at the end of the flock, carrying the wounded lamb in his arms along the dusty road.

As they neared the palace where the animals were to be sacrificially slaughtered, the townspeople watched the procession in the streets with delight and growing excitement. Who was this stranger – a saint, apparently – who was coming to the palace? Look, he himself carried a sacrificial lamb to the gods; clearly, it showed that he was honouring the sacrifice!

Some knew him as the holy man who dwelt with the rishis in the hills. Everyone had heard something of him and now that he was here, coming to the king, it was understandable that everyone was excited. Some even ran ahead to announce at the palace the approach of this saint; the king, hearing the news, was pleased that his sacrifice would be attended by a holy man

In the great chamber of the palace, the nobles and priests made way to let the future Buddha pass, for there was something awe-inspiring about him. How majestic, how quiet, how pleasing he was! Gautama stood and watched, as the Brahmin priests prepared to go about their bloody work.

Then a hush fell as a priest stepped forward, grasped a goat by its neck, and brought it close to the holy sacrificial flames. A long knife glittered in his hand as he offered up his prayer. "See, dreadful gods! See this goat brought for a sacrifice to please you! Take pleasure in its blood and in the smell of its roasting meat, as the fire consumes its flesh! Let the king's sins be laid upon this goat and let them be consumed as well, for now I strike!"

But at that moment, as he raised his knife, the future Buddha called out, "Let him not strike, great king!" And the knife halted in mid-air.

Gautama stepped up to the fettered goat and cut its bonds. None stopped him, such was his strength of purpose, his commanding presence. All eyes turned to the king, to see what he would do. It was King Bimbisara on the throne, the very ruler whom Gautama had met six years earlier, just after he renounced his princely life.

"Great king!" Gautama said, and Bimbisara listened respect-fully. "Let me speak of life and of its taking. For all can take it, but none can give it, and all creatures on earth strive to retain it.

"We are like gods to the animals, great king! They pay us tribute with their milk and wool and, when we slaughter them like this, we pay them back poorly indeed. Can we forget that we are taught that man may rise from such beasts and that he may cut short the journey of a being with such killing? We must not kill, not merely for pity's sake, but also lest we slay the meanest thing upon its upward way!

"And, let me ask, great king, why sacrifice to gods? If the gods are good and so compassionate, they will not want our bloody offerings; if they do not in fact exist, then the sacrifice is wasted; if they are evil, will the killing of a goat bribe them into doing good?"

So spoke Gautama at great length, telling of universal brotherhood, how all that lives is one, united in the bond of birth and life and death. He showed such gentleness, such compassion, and such great love that all were deeply moved. The chastised priests snuffed out the sacrificial fires and threw away their knives, and King Bimbisara paid the future Buddha reverence. And on the next day, the king issued a decree, forbidding all slaughter, whether for sacrifice or meat, and teaching all the people of his land that it was love and mercy, not blood, which brought down mercy to humankind.

King Bimbisara was moved to plead with Gautama to stay in the palace, to teach him wisdom. But the future Buddha knew his purpose and declined. "Noble king!" he said, "I shall return to you in love when I have found that which I seek! Truth exists and must be found!"

Then the future Buddha left the palace and the town and set his feet again towards Uruvela, still troubled, still seeking, never disheartened.

Near where Gautama was accustomed to meditate stood a bo-tree, a wild fig tree (*ficus religiosa*), a pipal. Because it was under this that he was to find enlightenment, it is called the Bodhi-tree (Tree of Enlightenment) and is revered by Buddhists everywhere. Such a tree is planted near each Buddhist temple and an ancient nine-story temple was later built to mark the site of the original, under which Gautama now seated himself.

This place, Uruvela, is now called Bodh-Gaya, and is in the state of Behar.

Here the future Buddha seated himself in the cross-legged lotus position. Dusk was approaching and the earth was growing quiet, as though expectantly. Gautama shut his eyes gently and, with all the resolution he could muster, uttered this oath: "Skin, sinew and bone may dry up as it will; my flesh and blood may dry in my body, but without attaining complete enlightenment I will not leave this seat."[14]

Seated Buddha

> He whose passions are stilled, who is not absorbed in
> enjoyment, who has perceived the Void, the
> Unconditioned, the Absolute, his path is difficult
> to understand, like that of birds in the ether.
>
> *The Dhammapada* (v. 93)

VI

The Night of Attainment

As darkness fell, the glittering moonlight fell upon Gautama's immobile body underneath the tree. Hardly could one note its breathing, so quiet was he; his back was as straight as the trunk of the tree itself and his body was stilled as only a man could still it who had endured as Gautama had endured during his years of effort. Within the stilled temple of his body, Gautama strove and was alert.

We may imagine his inner state as that of a mighty warrior, poised and keen for battle, standing within a great chariot which had come to an expectant but complete halt. This warrior needs not strain at the reins of unruly horses: he is their master and they do his bidding. His carriage has been checked, all repairs have been made, it is in working order, and it is still. Boldly the warrior stands, alert, awake, prepared for what is to come.

On this night in the year 528 BCE, the night of Gautama's thirty-fifth birthday, that vehicle was Gautama's body; within it, the future Buddha was quick, undistracted, and vital. And as his consciousness probed ever deeper within himself, seeking enlightenment, the onslaught came and the battle was joined.

Tradition speaks of the armies of Mara the tempter being loosed against the future Buddha that night, but these soldiers exist in all men and women; the battlefield which would be contested that night was within Gautama himself, although here we use the demons' names as given in the ancient texts.

78

Mara! This was no ordinary "devil", for Mara is negation, that which opposes, the force which rises within us when we seek to respond to the higher nature which calls us to follow it.* To Mara, the future Buddha was the incarnation of all this "Evil One" opposed and feared, for Gautama was striving to be the Awakened One, and therefore Mara's greatest threat. It is Mara who may be said to thrive on all that keeps us asleep within ourselves, and makes us the slaves of our appetites, emotions, and transient thoughts. It was no wonder then that, according to legend, Mara unleashed on that night of great effort every demon in his ranks, to break Gautama's will, his aim, his purpose. For only when there is effort does opposition – Mara – appear. Why need he come to the slothful, worldly man, contentedly asleep? As one scholar put it, "Mara knew that if the underlying reason for the unending cycle of death and rebirth were discovered, his power would be ruined. Hence, he struggled to thwart the achievement of Gautama's goal."[15]

First to attack Gautama was the Sin of Self, Egoism, the demon named *Attavada*. "If you are the enlightened one," *Attavada* said within Gautama's breast, "let it be enough that you attain enlightenment, Nirvana. Take the blessing for yourself!"

But the future Buddha recognised that voice. "You cheat those who love themselves," Gautama said. "Depart!" And *Attavada* slunk back into gloom.

Now came *Visikitcha* – Doubt – that mighty tempter.

"All is in vain, even this!" Doubt said, sneering at effort. "Look at all you have surrendered; what have you received in return? You gave up palaces, a noble name, a wife, a son, parents, six years of life – what has it brought you? So far, nothing! And why? Because nothing exists, your search is vain and useless, and your quest after Buddhahood is sheer presumption!"

"Most noble *Visikitcha*," Gautama said, " you are man's most treacherous foe, for you appear with cunning and reasonable

---

* From the Sanskrit *mri*, meaning "death".

words to make a man abandon effort. Yet begone, Doubt, for you have no part with me!"

Now Mara unleashed Scruple, which rose before the future Buddha's inner eye to whisper, "How dare you think yourself greater than those who wrote the Vedas? Who are you that you should cast doubt on priests and sacrifices? How dare you question all that wiser men have taught?"

But Gautama knew false *Silabbat-paramasa* for what it was. "You tie men to forms only, Witch!" he answered. "Truth is One and has nothing to do with outer forms like rites and sacrifices. Begone!"

The night grew darker now and storm clouds rose, created, it is said, by Mara. Before Gautama's eyes appeared the demon *Kamma*, king of passions, so mighty that even the gods bowed before his lures.

He drew his flower-bedecked bow and shot his five-pronged arrows at the future Buddha, reaching his five senses. He brought with him the most seductive maidens, haunting, voluptuous, such as mortal man had never seen, who danced before Gautama, beckoning him sweetly to find heaven in their arms. But Gautama sat alert, unmoved, and imperturbable, even when *Kamma* caused one of his maidens to appear before him in the lovely guise of Yasodhara, Gautama's bride, pleading with him to return home, to rest with her.

"False demons!" Gautama said, "just for her sake shall I remain here, as for the sake of all mankind." And the maidens vanished from Gautama's inner sight and Mara, the tempter, paused to prepare a fresh attack.

Hate led the renewed assault. She, *Patigha*, with her venomous snakes coiling about her waist, is said to have been swiftly repulsed by Gautama's calm and level gaze; next came *Ruparaga*, Lust of Days, that which causes man not only to cling ignobly to mortal life but to wish for another after death; next, *Aruparaga*, Lust of Fame; then *Mano*, Fiend of Pride; next *Uddhachcha*, who was Self-Righteousness; then Ignorance, and a score more.

Resolute in purpose and in wakefulness within, Gautama vanquished each as it arose. He purified himself that night, meeting unflinchingly those lusts and demons most of us spend our lives trying to deny, escape, or to ignore.

He never slackened, though his fight was won. Now that he had been cleansed through his own efforts, his army of demons, which all human beings contain, was stilled, and he might now approach the great task with greater lightness. As a warrior discards all that impedes his chariot's swiftness, so had the future Buddha rid himself of the dominance of all that which defiles man's nature and readied himself to seize the ultimate prize in the greatest struggle of them all.

How could he have approached enlightenment – truth – if he had still been subject to doubt, pride, ignorance, self-righteousness, and lusts? Such ordinary baggage would not serve the coming journey. For the path which Gautama would now tread, he needed to be light, quick, alert and wide awake.

So was the future Buddha now, as the first watch of the night approached. His meditation deepened, to reach a depth which, it is said, is unfathomable to those who have not attained Buddhahood. In this state, Gautama is said to have perceived the five hundred and fifty lives through which he had lived in ages past. It was as though he, the traveller, stood on a mountaintop and overlooked the gorges, valleys, crevasses, and swamps over which he had walked before he came to this point. He saw also how all was just and lawful: how good brought forth more good, and evil brought forth more evil in new lives; how every act is written down and totalled at a man's life's end, to spell his future fate. Past thoughts and deeds, wishes, strivings, everything remained, nothing was lost; each cause had its effect, each new effect was in itself a new cause.*

Then in the middle watch of that fateful night, the future Buddha attained the state called *Abinna*, wherein his consciousness and understanding rose to all the Universe. It is written that

---

* *Karma*, which Christmas Humphreys called the "law of laws".

he saw – and what is more, understood – the lawful working of the sun and planets, of all the solar systems, of all galaxies; he saw worlds upon worlds, those which were and those which are yet to be, aeons hence; saw how they arose, thrived, and were destroyed; saw all the Great Laws at work. And seeing the Great Laws, he saw their application here on earth as well; understood the place of humankind in them, knew the place of every living thing.

No longer did he wonder why the shrike killed other living creatures, why tigers killed, why all that lives feeds on another, why farmers laboured to bring forth produce watered in their sweat, why death occurred, and pain and illness too. He saw that Great Laws must be obeyed and are best served willingly, humbly and with cheer.

Then came the last watch of the night and still the future Buddha sat, unmoved ever since he had seated himself upon his grassy cushion underneath the tree. Now, in his last, supreme, inner effort, it is said that his mind tore veil upon veil away from the highest mysteries, as his spirit soared ever higher and higher in planes of consciousness undreamt of by man. And, having reached the "supreme, complete enlightenment", the highest level of consciousness attainable, Gautama perceived the cause of suffering and the way to escape from suffering.

He now understood what he was to call the Four Noble Truths, the foundation of the *Dhamma* (in the Pali, or in Sanskrit, *Dharma*) – the Law, the Truth. There was, he saw, not only suffering on earth, but also a specific cause of suffering. This was craving – the clinging to desires – in all sorts of large and subtle ways, even to life, even to the wish for an after-life. Not to receive what one desires is suffering, and to receive that which one does not desire is suffering too, this Gautama perceived. He saw that craving chains man to the object of his desire, makes him its slave, and causes him to suffer. He saw that the craving for life on earth and for life after death created the *karma* which created new lives and these, in turn, were a perpetuation of new suffering. He saw that man carries suffering about with him always, as a wheel travels with the carriage, and that it is only delusion which closes his eyes to this reality. He saw that suffering abides even in pleasures and delights – in the recognition of their impermanence, for they are here today and gone tomorrow.

Not only did Gautama perceive that there was suffering and an origin of suffering, but he saw also the third Noble Truth – that there is a cure for suffering. And this truth about the cessation of suffering led Gautama to perceive the fourth Noble Truth: that the way lay in what he called the Noble Eightfold Path.

The Four Noble Truths and the Noble Eightfold Path! Gautama had come to the ultimate answers and, in arriving at them, he perceived the Wheel of the Law which explains all human existence and the round of rebirths.

It is said that it was in this supreme moment of illumination that Prince Siddhartha Gautama achieved complete Buddhahood, became the Buddha, the Enlightened One, the Awakened One, the Illumined One – or, as he often called himself, the Tathagata.

His enlightenment had been spread over three watches of the night, or about nine hours, and was a gradual process involving extreme mental clarity. Guided by reason, he is said then to have reached omniscience, perfect knowledge, to have destroyed in himself the roots of rebirth, having attained to the highest levels of consciousness, the highest bliss, to Nirvana!

Indeed, the realisation arose in him: "Rebirth [for me] is destroyed, I have completed the holy life, done is what had to be done, there is no more of being for me!" Whereupon the Buddha cried out in joy:

> "My emancipation is assured,
> This is my last birth,
> There will be no more re-becoming!"[16]

The Buddha – for now he would be known by that name – rested under the Bodhi-tree for seven days (seven weeks, some sources say) after reaching Enlightenment. Then, it is said, Mara assailed him one more time. It is enough, he told the Buddha, that you have attained your goal; others will not understand your teaching, your "Way", for they are deep in the sleep of delusion and are satisfied with the passing trifles of life. Do not waste your time on them; you will only be vexed! The road before you will be wearisome, Mara whispered, and trying to enlighten mankind will be useless.

Within the Buddha's heart, Mara insinuated that, having achieved Buddhahood, he might now choose *Parinirvana* – total Nirvana – choose to die to the highest bliss, from that moment on never needing to reappear. There was nothing more for the Buddha to achieve for himself in life: why not leave it? The battle is won and the victor leaves the field of carnage; he does not loiter about, trying to help corpses!

The Buddha pondered and then came to his compassionate decision. He decided that it is indeed true that men have eyes to see, but see not; that they have ears to hear, but hear not; that it will be difficult for them to perceive his *Dhamma*, as the caged bird often shuns the open door to freedom.

Yet, still, there may be some who are troubled enough to search for an answer to the mysteries of life and intelligent enough to comprehend it: even if these are the very, very few, still he must teach the Way to them. And (as he came to be known) the All-Enlightened One – the All-Compassionate One too – made up his mind.

"Yea, I preach!" he said. "Who so will listen let him learn the Law!"

"To whom shall I first announce the Dhamma?" he asked himself. Briefly, he wished he had a teacher to advise him, but then it came to him that he must conquer his hesitation and make the teaching, the Dhamma itself, his master.

In his mind appeared an image which helped him understand what it was that he must do and to whom he must preach.*

* His very first converts are said to have been two merchants, Tapussa and Bhallika, travellers in a caravan, who happened upon him at this point and offered him barley gruel and honey as food. Their gift having been accepted, they are said to have taken "refuge in the Buddha and the Dhamma" (which the Buddha had not yet promulgated), receiving from the Buddha in turn nail parings and locks of his hair. These men became the first lay followers of the Buddha.

He saw a pool filled with lotus plants. Some of their flowers were so deeply immersed in water that they would never reach the surface; others were already upright and flowering in full light, while yet others were almost on the surface of the water. The first, the Buddha saw, would never bloom, the second had already reached their goal, while the third could, if assisted, blossom.

Humanity, too, could be divided into similar groups, he reasoned. Some were prisoners of error and false teachings; others had achieved their goal and found the truth; a third group were still confused and sought the true path.

The latter contained many who were hesitant about which way to follow. They needed help; compassionately, the Buddha decided he would teach the law to them.[17]

But the Dhamma, he realised, was difficult to grasp, however necessary it was for all human beings. He must first, therefore, teach it to those best prepared to comprehend it quickly, to those who by dint of their spiritual self-training had already achieved great knowledge – to his former teachers, Alara Kalapa and Uddaka, the disciple of Rama. But then the knowledge came to him that each had died, the first a week ago, the latter the previous night.

"Nobly born they were," the Buddha thought with compassion. "If they had heard the Law they would swiftly have comprehended it."

Next, the Buddha thought of the five disciples who had attended him for many years. True, they had left him in disgust when, to their dismay, he had turned from the path of extreme asceticism, but he knew them to be sincere and learned.

"What if I should first declare the Dhamma to the five mendicants?" the Buddha asked himself, and then arose, gathered up his robes and begging bowl, and started on his way.

If you see an intelligent man who tells you where true
treasures are to be found, who shows what is to be
avoided, and who administers reproofs, follow
that wise man; it will be better, not worse, for
those who follow him.

The Dhammapada (v. 76)

VII

The First Turning of the
Wheel of the Law

IN THE DEER PARK AT ISIPATANA, near the city of Benares, sat
Kondanna, the eldest of the five monks, together with
Bhaddiya, Vappa, Mahanama, and Assaji. Since they had left
Gautama, they had stayed there, meditating and following the way
of asceticism which they felt Gautama had abandoned in abject
fashion. On that particular day, they were again together, having
come from the town where they had begged the merest scraps of
food, and were seated now, silent and attentive.

Perhaps they heard soft footsteps; perhaps a rustle of the grass
came to their ears; in any case, something caused them to turn
their heads.

With what amazement did they note their old friend Gautama
approaching! They hardly recognised him. The body which they
knew as wasted, shrivelled, and dried, had recovered; it shone like
gold in the sunlight, its skin was sleek and beautiful like a charger's
after a race has been won, and Gautama's pace was strong and
majestic, like a king conscious of his power. Despite that, they
briefly clung to their preconceptions.

"Look who approaches!" they whispered. "Here comes the
devotee Gautama, who lives in comfort, who lives in plenty, who

has given up the effort, and has turned to a life of ease! We shall prepare a place for him out of courtesy, but it would not be fitting for us to rise or salute him, or take his bowl or robe. If he wishes to sit down with us, let him, but it will be no pleasure for us to have him here!"

As the Buddha approached, however, none of them could abide by that decision. For they had perceived something distinctly different about him, something commanding respect, something higher. And in this they showed the developed state of their own understanding, for it requires a higher understanding to perceive that which is in itself higher. Lacking understanding, the spiritually-low scoff, mock, and scorn, but these five monks had eyes to see – and saw; they had ears to hear – and understood. One of them took the Buddha's begging bowl and robe; another assigned a place for him to sit, and another brought water to wash his feet, dusty from the long walk to Benares.

Still, in addressing him, they used the familiar "Friend" or "Brother Gautama," only to have the Buddha correct them. Quite simply, as one states a fact, the Buddha told them not to address him in such a familiar fashion.

"Know that the Immortal has been attained. I am the Buddha, the Tathagata. I teach, I show the Law," he said. "Follow it and you shall obtain deliverance!"

They had to admit they had never before heard him speak in this way. They listened, though still sceptical, as he proceeded to preach his first sermon.

And when he had finished, the eyes of the five monks were opened. First, Kondanna embraced the Dhamma, and was henceforth called "*Anata*," meaning "He Who Has Understood." And soon the other four were brought to understand the Dhamma, perceiving its merit. Thus, these five – and, of course, the Buddha himself – became the first monks (*bhikkhus*) in the Buddhist order of monks (*sangha*) which persists to this day.

This first sermon or, as Buddhists call it, this discourse (*sutta*), comprises the basic teaching of Buddhism, its message to humanity. It is referred to variously as the "sermon at Benares" or as "The First Turning of the Wheel of the Doctrine." This Wheel came to be a symbol of Buddhism itself and is today even a part of the national emblem of the Republic of India. So basic is it that many Indian sculptures depicting the life of the Buddha do not show him physically, but represent him by the Wheel itself.

Of the countless recorded discourses given by the Buddha to his followers in the forty-five years of his ministry, none are as central to Buddhism as is this first sermon, which set forth what the Buddha called the Four Noble Truths and the Noble Eightfold Path. It comprises the essence of Buddhism and is all that is required for a man to follow in the Way of the Buddha. As a teaching, it was revolutionary when it was first proclaimed; it remains so today.

"Never in the history of the world had a scheme of salvation been put forth so simple in its nature, so free from any superhuman agency, so independent of, so even antagonistic to the belief in a soul, the belief in God, and the hope for a future life," wrote the nineteenth century scholar Rhys Davids.[18] "...it was a turning-point in the religious history of man when a reformer, full of the most earnest moral purpose, and trained in all the intellectual culture of his time, put forth deliberately, and with a knowledge of the opposing views, the doctrine of a salvation to be found here, in this life, in an inward change of heart, to be brought about by perseverance in a mere system of self-culture and of self-control."

In words which various ancient Pali texts attribute to the Buddha himself, here is what the Buddha taught that day in the deer park at Isipatana:

"Hear, O monks! I teach the Middle Way. There are two ways not to be followed: the pursuit of desires and of the pleasure which springs from desire on the one hand, and the pursuit of pain and hardship on the other.

"For the first is base, common, ignoble, unprofitable, and leading to rebirth, while the way of self-mortification is grievous, ignoble, and also unprofitable.

"What are the characteristics of the Middle Way?

"It avoids both these extremes. It is enlightened, brings clear vision, makes for wisdom, and leads to peace, insight, enlightenment, and Nirvana.

"The Middle Way is the Noble Eightfold Path: right understanding; right attitude of mind; right speech; right conduct; right livelihood; right effort; right attentiveness, and right meditation. This is the Middle Way.

"Now, what are the Four Noble Truths?

"This is the first – the Noble Truth of Suffering. Birth, age, disease, death – all these are suffering; contact with the unpleasant is suffering; separation from the pleasant is suffering; every wish unfulfilled is suffering; all the five components of the individuality are suffering. And these are the five components of the individuality: forms, perceptions, sensations, psychic dispositions, and consciousness.

"This is the second – the Noble Truth of the Arising of Suffering: it arises from craving, which leads to rebirth, which brings delight and passion, and seeks pleasure now here, now there – the craving after sensual pleasure, for continued life, for power.

"This is the third – the Noble Truth of the Cessation of Suffering: it is the complete stopping of that craving, so that no passion, no clinging, remains. It lies in leaving craving, in being freed of it, in being released from it, in giving it no place in oneself.

"And this is the fourth – the Noble Truth of the Way which leads to the Cessation of Suffering: it is the Noble Eightfold Path, already stated."

What did the Buddha mean by suffering and by craving (often misinterpreted as "desire")? His meaning is important to us, if we are not to misunderstand the nature of this great teaching. For many a Westerner has considered Buddhism "pessimistic" simply because he has misunderstood what Buddhists mean by the words "suffering" and "craving".

The late Christmas Humphreys, author of many books on Buddhism and founder-president of The Buddhist Society, London, explained as follows:

"...'suffering' is only one translation of the Pali *dukkha*, which covers all that we understand by pain, ill, disease – physical and mental – including such minor forms as disharmony, discomfort, irritation or friction, or, in a philosophic sense, the awareness of incompleteness or insufficiency. It is dissatisfaction and discontent, the opposite of all that we embrace in the terms well-being, perfection, wholeness, bliss."[19]

Buddhism is not pessimistic; it is realistic. It does not, for example, deny that spiritual or material happiness exists; it simply points to their impermanent and therefore imperfect nature.

What remains after craving – which causes suffering – is eliminated? The answer is implied by the above: a perfected state of well-being, wholeness, bliss. The Buddhist strives after these; he strives after serenity, tranquillity, after an inner balance which accompanies inner self-mastery.

Desire, says the Buddhist, springs from and is caused by ignorance – and the clinging to desire the Buddhist calls *craving*. It springs up when a man is ignorant of the fact that everything is transient, temporary, impermanent, changing.

Whatever we see, says the Buddhist, either within or outside ourselves, to all this can we say: "This does not belong to me; this am I not; this is not my Ego."

In the words of the Buddha:

"Just as one calls *hut* the circumscribed space which comes to be by means of wood and rushes, reeds and clay, even so we call body the circumscribed space that comes to be by means of bones and sinews, flesh and skin ...

"Suppose a man, who can see, were to behold the many bubbles on the Ganges [river] as they are driving along. And he should watch them and carefully examine them. After carefully examining them, they will appear to him as empty, unreal, and insubstantial. In exactly the same way does the monk behold all the bodily forms, feelings, perceptions, mental formations, and states of consciousness – whether they be of the past, or the present, or the future, far or near. And he watches them and examines them carefully, and, after carefully examining them, they appear to him as empty, void, and without Ego ..."

Desires arise in man, but in truth, says the Buddhist, they are insubstantial, empty, unreal, impermanent, changing, transient. Yet the ignorant man, who does not perceive this, craves after the objects of desire, which are themselves equally impermanent, changing, transient, insubstantial, and unreal.

The Buddha taught that it was in this craving, in this *attachment to desires*, that the root of suffering is to be found. Trying to satisfy desire is simply "beating one's head against the wall," for desire buffets a man about, causing him to chase now here, now there; now after this, now after that, like a man bereft of his senses. Desire, says the Buddhist, leads the man and makes a slave of him: in all this lies suffering.

Freedom – and thus ultimately the highest bliss, Nirvana – comes to a man, said the Buddha, when he has snuffed out cravings by eliminating ignorance. And the Buddha had a positive, hopeful, teaching to offer in this respect, for the Noble Eightfold Path is practical and substantial. It is, in the words of Buddhists, a "come-and-see-way" which a man may try to his great benefit.

No priests, *gurus* or teachers are needed to follow this path; each Buddhist must serve as his own teacher, for Buddha taught a personal teaching in which nothing must be believed which does not make good sense to the individual. Buddhism is in fact a teaching without a formal creed, for even the Noble Eightfold Path and the Four Noble Truths are only guides, to be tested and confirmed by the individual man and woman.

What is the Noble Eightfold Path? Again, we shall go back to the original words of the Buddha to examine each step upon it.

It begins with Right Understanding. This means to understand the Four Noble Truths: to understand the existence of suffering; to understand how it arises; to understand how it may be ended, and to understand the Path which leads to the extinction of suffering.

It includes, further, a right understanding of what the Buddha called the "Five Aggregates of Existence," namely, the nature of bodily forms, feelings, perceptions, mental formations, and consciousness, and it also means a right understanding of the roots of merit and demerit.

Greed, anger, and delusion, the Buddha taught, are roots of demerit; their absence is the root of merit. Merit and demerit themselves he defined in the following way. Demerit includes the destruction of living things; stealing; unlawful sexual intercourse; lying; tale-bearing; harsh language; frivolous talk; covetousness; ill-will, and wrong views. Abstaining from these constitute what the Buddha calls merit.

Right attitude of mind implies right motive. In following the Noble Eightfold Path, the Buddhist is vitally concerned with motive. It includes "right aim" or "intention" and implies a strong desire not to follow the cravings of the impermanent "self" and a wish to relieve the suffering of mankind.

Right attitudes of mind (or, as it is sometimes called, "right-mindedness") means turning one's mind away from worldly matters and directing it attentively to overcoming evil-mindedness. Thus it brings into play three forces: right understanding, right effort, and right attentiveness.

Now advice follows on how such right-mindedness is to be applied to daily life. He who follows the Path avoids lying, tale-bearing, harsh language and frivolous or vain talk. How does he speak? The Buddha answers:

"He speaks the truth, is devoted to the truth, reliable, worthy of confidence, is not a deceiver of men... He never knowingly speaks a lie, neither for the sake of his own advantage, nor for the sake of another person's advantage, nor for the sake of any advantage whatsoever.

"He abstains from tale-bearing. What he has heard here, he does not repeat there, so as to cause dissension there; and what he has heard there, he does not repeat here, so as to cause dissension here. Thus he unites those who are divided, and those who are united he encourages. Concord gladdens him and it is concord that he spreads by his words.

"He abstains from harsh language, speaks words that are gentle, soothing to the ear, loving, going to the heart, courteous and dear, and agreeable to many.

"He abstains from vain talk. He speaks at the right time, in accordance with facts, speaks what is useful, speaks about the law and the discipline; his speech is like a treasure, at the right moment accompanied by arguments, moderate and full of sense."

Having described Right Speech, the Buddha next described the fourth step on the Noble Eightfold Path, this being Right Conduct or Right Action.

"[He] avoids the killing of living beings and abstains from it," the Buddha said. "Without stick or sword, conscientious, full of sympathy, he is anxious for the welfare of all living beings.

"He avoids stealing and abstains from it; avoids unlawful sexual intercourse, and abstains from it; avoids lying, slander, and deceit, and he avoids wasting his energy in slothfulness or worldly enjoyments ..."

These are called the Five Precepts, constituting a moral law, or ethic. The Buddhist realises that Action is two-fold: it is made up of that which we do and that which we refrain from doing, or do not do. Also, the Buddhist knows that action can go on in the mind and that wrong actions are none the less harmful because they never left that secret place.

As Christmas Humphreys put it, "Murder is none the less murder in that it never left the heart, and a slanderous thought is as harmful to its thinker and his enemies as any spoken word. Again, it is possible to get drunk on excitement; theft is no less theft because it wears the cloak of custom, and a lustful thought befouls its owner's purity."[20]

Under Right Action or Conduct is included the all-important matter of self-control. The Buddha always enjoined his followers to be "well-controlled," for how else can these precepts be followed?

The first precept, regarding the killing of living things, seems obvious. Yet the Buddhist never went along with mankind's comfortable inconsistencies here, for he rejects killing, for example, for sport or personal adornment. He would not think highly of assassinating animals so that their heads or skins may ultimately adorn someone's home, nor would he think highly of fashions which would have us wrap ourselves in the hides of dead animals.

Killing for sport or personal adornment is unnecessary and therefore demeritorious, said the Buddha. This idea, happily, has become fashionable in Western thinking today. Yet Buddhism suggests it is necessary for each of us to evaluate each situation in the light of common sense and compassionate regard for other living beings. While compassion for life would deter the Buddhist from countenancing the killing of animals, even for food, vegetarianism (which is central to Brahmanism) is not central to Buddhism, for the Buddha insisted that his disciples eat whatever is given them in their begging bowls, out of gratitude and courtesy to the giver. The Buddhist prefers doing without meat or fish for food, but as being considerate of others is the important consideration, a Buddhist might well wish, for example, to serve meat at his own table, if his guest were a meat-eater. The Buddha permitted his disciples to eat "whatever food it is customary to eat in any place or country provided it is done without indulgence of the appetites, or evil desires."[21]

Motive, he cautioned, is all-important, not only here, but also concerning money matters. Stealing is forbidden, and the Buddhist sees through our contemporary, usually lax, business ethics. He would certainly regard many a "sharp business deal" as stealing; similarly, the employee who does not give his employer honest work for his wages steals from him as surely as he would if he were to take cash. As for amassing money, the Buddha himself often told the rich men of his day that it is not life and wealth and power which enslave a man – but the clinging to them. "He who possesses wealth and uses it rightly will be a blessing unto his fellow-beings," said the Buddha.

"Of all the lusts and desires," says the Buddha, "there is none so powerful as sexual inclination." Sexual desire, the Buddha taught, is natural and not to be condemned, so long as it is rightly-controlled. As we think, so we are, and the Buddha taught that our attitudes, or motives, govern the nature of this part of our life as well. Indulging in lustful thoughts or emotions befouls the individual and does violence to the object of desire, teaches the Buddha. Again, "the disciples of the Buddha are always well-controlled."

In the fourth precept, the Buddha cautions the individual against lies, slander, and deceit. Although this is covered in "Right Speech," the third step along the Noble Eightfold Path, it is re-emphasised here. Once more, Buddhists recognise that lying, slander, and deceit need not leave the heart or tongue to cause their damage.

The Buddha, after all, is advising his disciples about their own "inner growth" and the person in whose heart slander mutters its poison finds that it obstructs his path. Certainly, this precept covers idle gossip, as it does malicious gossip; it covers all forms of boasting, maliciously withholding facts, and false advice.

In the last of the Buddha's five precepts, he cautions us against seeking or stimulating excitement with the aid of drugs or drink, against squandering our inner strength and power either through stimulation or laziness. He urges a right use of one's energies, so necessary to maintain perfect control. Just as the lazy man cannot climb the upward way of the Path, neither can he whose being is befuddled with alcohol or drugs. Those who chase after artificial excitements will not find time to perfect themselves, nor the energy with which to engage in the task; they cannot free themselves from bondage. The Buddhist might well point out that we cannot be mentally alert while slouching passively before a television screen, nor inwardly active, in pursuit of the great goal, if our minds dwell only on finding new ways of being entertained. Further, there is no "boredom" for a person on a spiritual quest – and certainly no wish to "kill time."

As to Right Livelihood, the Buddha left this question largely to the common sense of the individual. He states only that right livelihood means avoiding wrong livelihood; a person should follow an occupation which is in harmony with the Five Precepts and the ethical portions of the Noble Eightfold Path. It is up to each of us to examine our own way of making a living, to see whether that way is in harmony with the Path.

Does our occupation require us to lie? If so, then Buddhism would ask us to resolve that problem somehow for ourselves, either by refraining from lying or by leaving this type of work. Is it more fitting to be a gardener than a worker in a slaughterhouse? The answer is clear, to the Buddhist. For each of us, the answer must be personal: if we are honest with ourselves, we will be able to gauge our work objectively, to see whether it furthers the welfare of humanity or hinders it, whether it heals or causes suffering.

"There are Four Great Efforts," said the Buddha. "The effort to avoid; the effort to overcome; the effort to develop, and the effort to maintain.

"What now is the effort to avoid?" he asked, answering, "There the disciple incites his mind to avoid the arising of evil, demeritorious things, that have not yet arisen; and he strives, puts forth his energy, strains his mind and struggles.

"Thus, when he perceives a form with the eye, a sound with the ear, an odour with the nose, a taste with the tongue, a contact with the body, or an object with the mind, he neither adheres to the whole, nor to its parts. And he strives to ward off that, through which evil and demeritorious things, greed and sorrow, would arise, if he remained with unguarded senses; and he watches over his senses, restrains his senses.

"Possessed of this noble control over the senses, he experiences inwardly a feeling of joy, into which no evil thing can enter. This is called the effort to avoid."

The effort to overcome needs to be made when evil, demeritorious thoughts have already arisen. In such a case, the Buddha says, there are five things an individual can do.

If such thoughts have arisen by means of an object which has been perceived by one of the six senses (the Buddhist regards the mind as the sixth sense), then one may use this very object to gain another and wholesome object.

What the Buddha meant here may be explained by the advice he gave to those men in whom lustful thoughts enter upon seeing a woman: if she is honourable, let him think of her as his sister; if she is old, let him think of her as his mother; if she is of small account, let her be regarded as a younger sister, etc. Here the object (the woman), which has prompted the demeritorious thoughts, can be used to gain a wholesome object (sister, mother) for the mind.

Or, the man should reflect on the nature of these thoughts, saying, "unwholesome are these thoughts, blameable are these thoughts, of painful result are these thoughts!"

Or, he should pay no attention to these thoughts, paying them no heed, turning away from them.

Or, he should consider the compounded nature of these thoughts (of what they are made; that they are impermanent, insubstantial, unreal).

Or, finally, "with teeth clenched... he should restrain, suppress, and root out these thoughts; and in doing so, these evil and demeritorious thoughts of greed, anger, and delusion will dissolve and disappear, and the mind will inwardly become settled and calm, composed and concentrated." This, said the Buddha, is called the effort to overcome.

"What now," he asks, "is the effort to develop?

"There the disciple incites the will to arouse meritorious conditions, that have not yet arisen," the Buddha explained, "and he strives, puts forth his energy, strains his mind and struggles."

By doing so, the individual develops the so-called Elements of Enlightenment – namely, Attentiveness, Investigation of the Law, Energy, Rapture, Tranquillity, Concentration, and Equanimity. This, said the Buddha, is called the effort to develop.

As for the effort to maintain, the Buddha said, "There the disciple incites his will to maintain the meritorious conditions that have already arisen, and not to let them disappear, but to bring them to growth, to maturity, and to the full perfection of development; and he strives, puts forth his energy, strains his mind and struggles. This is called the effort to maintain."

How very different a picture such Right Effort gives us of the inner state of the Buddhist, from that of which we have perhaps heard before! How mistaken are those who have been taught to regard the contemplative, meditative individual as "inactive, passive, apathetic, lethargic, dreamy"!

We have seen what the Buddha meant by Right Effort. He asks his followers to be awake – inwardly vital, vibrantly alive, alert, attentive. Of course, this state has nothing in common with the restless activity, the thrashing about, which the West so often confuses with vitality. Here, there is striving and struggling always – and how could it be otherwise? The Buddha taught that help from gods or priests is not to be sought, that his followers must rely only on themselves. Prayers won't do, nor can magic sacrifices bring enlightenment; everything is ultimately left to the individual man and woman.

The very last words of the Buddha, before he died, might be cited here. "Work out your own salvation with diligence!" he told his monks – and then said no more. "To work" – and to do so "with diligence" – without these nothing can be obtained along the path of Gautama Buddha.

The Buddha's "Noble Eightfold Path" now gets steeper. The first two steps dealt with a correct understanding of the Dhamma; the next three with ordering one's life, life-habits, and life-ways so as to make the inner journey possible; now the seventh and eighth concern themselves with the greatest efforts.

The seventh step, Right Attentiveness, deals with a system of inner discipline, with techniques virtually unknown in the West except through Eastern sources. They are meant to make man the master of his mind, not its slave; this is an Eastern ideal, basic to Buddhism as it is to other systems such as Yoga too.

Yoga means "yoke" and, just as oxen are harnessed to a yoke, so does the yogi* harness his inner life, putting it under control. Many Westerners have considered the techniques of Yoga extremely valuable to men of all lands; one such is the Christian author of an unusual book on the discipline.

"In the East," he wrote, "there exists a large group of thoroughly tested techniques that could be termed the way or path of silence.

* meaning simply one who practices Yoga

From distant times, sages in India have been teaching men to keep mastery over their thoughts, to control their psychic being, and to establish themselves in an atmosphere of relaxation and profound peace, far from everything 'noising' in man and around him…"[22]

It is these "thoroughly tested" techniques which the Buddha twenty-five centuries ago dealt with in explaining the seventh step of his Noble Eightfold Path. While he did not teach yoga, he did teach principles of awareness and attention which were known to the yogis of his day as they are still known today.

The disciple, the Buddha says, is aware of and attentive to his body, his feelings, his mind, and to phenomena. To these four, he is "clearly conscious and attentive, after putting away worldly greed and grief" – that is, after having mastered the first six steps along the Path.

What does it mean for the disciple to be attentive to his body, to "dwell in contemplation of his body"? What is such attentiveness like, how is it practised, and what results may be gained?

The Buddhist is meant to be aware of his body's parts, attributes, and functions – as they arise and as they disappear. He does not merely "remember" that he sat down, moved about, inhaled and exhaled, etc. He is aware of doing so, at the time it occurs.

This is not easy. Our days, our very lives, seem to pass by as though in a dream: where were we when all the events of our day occurred? The Buddhist disciple, for one, is urged to be *there*. In the words of the Buddha, "When making a long exhalation, he knows: I make a long exhalation…"

Knowing does not mean "thinking about"; it is *awareness*. "Thus he dwells," says the Buddha, "in contemplation of the body, either with regard to his own person, or to other persons, or to both. He beholds how the body arises; beholds how it passes away; beholds the arising and passing away of the body. A body is there – this clear consciousness is present in him, because of his knowledge and mindfulness, and he lives independent, unattached to anything in the world. Thus does the disciple dwell in contemplation of the body."

What may be expected from such contemplation of the body if, as the Buddha says, "it is practised, developed, often repeated, has become one's habit, one's foundation, is firmly established, strengthened, and well-perfected?"

The Buddha states that one gains mastery over delight and discontent, over fear and anxiety; that one is not overcome by these states, but subdues them as they arise. In addition, he says, one gains mastery over cold, heat, hunger, thirst, malicious and wicked speech, bodily discomfort and pain, even unto death.

How can fear and anxiety be mastered by contemplating one's body? Perhaps the answer is implied in the writings of someone who studied many of the same questions which concerned the Indian sages. The English writer and editor, A. R. Orage, a pupil of G. I. Gurdjieff, dealt with the psychological states which invade us to take temporary possession of our bodies, assuming mastery over us. How can one deal with anger, short temper, fear and anxiety, he asks?

"When in, or in the process of developing, a black mood, observe and notice *only your physical states*," writes Orage. "Your body at such times is very eloquent; it exhibits a special set of symptoms for every mood. Observe and notice, as a matter of personal and scientific curiosity, how your body manifests this, that, or the other black mood. For instance, your mouth may go dry or there may be an unpleasant taste in it. Your skin may wrinkle; some of your muscles may contract; you may have indigestion, nausea, or a heavy weight near the heart. Scores of symptoms reveal themselves. If you simply observe, notice and enumerate them, as if you were reporting them for a novel or a textbook on psychology, by the time you have finished, your black mood will have disappeared. You will have saved its energy to make observations with."[23]

What is often called "inner separation" takes place in the process described by the Buddha – and by the Englishman quoted above.

The Buddha does not suggest that we should not have fear and anxiety, delight or discontent, physical discomfort, or experience sensations of cold, heat, hunger, thirst, or pain. Usually, we have no choice in the matter. Yet "right contemplation" can, he teaches, free us from slavery to these inner occurrences and enable us to deal with them as they arise, by not giving over all our energy to them. We have reserved some attentiveness for contemplation.

It seems significant that the Buddha listed fear, anxiety, delight, and discontent together with bodily discomforts. In so doing, he classified them as virtual physical ills – and of course we know that negative psychic states can ravage the human body.

But the Buddha also urges his disciple to be attentive to his feelings. He observes his feelings in the same way, through the method already stated, that of "inner separation," of not giving the feelings all one's energy, and thus of not being completely their slave.

How often we regret too late that we have "given in" to our emotions! How much human suffering is caused by such constant surrender – and its subsequent justification! Yet the Buddha does not urge the repression of emotions, nor does he recommend a ferocious denial of such emotions. He urges us instead to reserve part of our energy – and, thereby, of ourselves – to the observance of feelings, as they arise and as they fade away.

He says that the disciple, if he has an agreeable feeling, knows, "I have an agreeable feeling"; if he has a disagreeable feeling, he knows, "I have a disagreeable feeling," and, if he has an indifferent feeling, he knows, "I have an indifferent feeling."

What is meant here? What is meant by *he knows* – and why is such "knowing" of value?

Before there can be "a knower" in us, something that knows, we need to make an effort so that all our energy is not in the feeling itself, so that it has not drawn off all our attention. The Buddhist is urged to keep part of himself free of the feeling, so as to observe it, to contemplate it, to "know it."

Thus he sees it as it arises and as it fades away. Because he sees it, he also perceives, this feeling is impermanent; it is not "I".

A powerful action takes place when the disciple realises, "There is anger in me" rather than "I am angry!" When we think of ourselves as *being angry*, we confuse ourselves with the anger inhabiting us at the time; we have failed to perceive the impermanence, insubstantiality, and transient nature of our angry state.

Having confused that state with ourselves, having "identified" ourselves with it, we tend to justify our anger; and quickly find no end of reasons why that anger is understandable, inevitable, "normal", right and even nobly inspired. But when we note that there "is anger in me", we see the matter quite differently; we know, as the Buddha says, that something called anger arises and fades away in us, just as agreeable, disagreeable, and indifferent feelings will similarly arise and fade away.

Once more, the Buddha urges the disciple to take the same action towards his mind. Thus the disciple practices "inner separation" towards his mind; is not wholly enslaved by the state inhabiting his mind; is not wholly the servant of his mind.

In the words of the Buddha, such a person knows the composed mind as composed and the scattered mind as scattered, knows the greedy mind as greedy and the not-greedy mind as not-greedy, etc. Whatever kind of mind inhabits him at the moment, this he observes, contemplates, and thus is not completely dominated.

"Because of his knowledge and mindfulness," says the Buddha, the disciple "lives independent, unattached to anything in the world."

In Right Contemplation, the disciple observes yet other things, namely phenomena. He does this, says the Buddha, by what he called the Five Hindrances.

Lust – anger – torpor and drowsiness – restlessness and mental worry – and doubts –these are truly hindrances along man's path to peace and wisdom. The Buddhist is meant to know them for what they are, having been attentive to their arising and their passing away; he knows how they come to arise, how they are overcome, and is taught that they do not arise again, once they have been overcome.

And, further, the disciple is attentive to what the Buddha terms the Five Aggregates of Existence: bodily form, feeling, perception, mental formations, and consciousness. He sees how these also arise and fade away. He knows them as impermanent, ever-changing, not independent.

Moreover, says the Buddha, the disciple is also attentive to the seven Elements of Enlightenment, and contemplates them. He knows when there is in him attentiveness, investigation of the law, enthusiasm, tranquillity, concentration, equanimity, and he knows when these are not in him, how they come to arise, and also how they may be fully developed.

The Buddhist disciple is meant to contemplate and come to know one more set of phenomena, which the Buddha called the Six Subjective-Objective Sense-Factors. These are eye and forms; ear and sounds; nose and smells; tongue and tastes; body and touches, and mind and ideas – the "five senses" known to the West, with the addition of a sixth, mind and ideas.

Regarding these phenomena, the Buddha says the disciple "knows the fetter that arises in dependence on them" and "how the fetter came to arise, how the fetter is overcome, and how the abandoned fetter does not rise again in the future."

That fetter, which makes slaves of us all, is attachment – that is, craving. In the abandonment of that fetter lies bliss – and, ultimately, even Nirvana.

All human beings, the Buddha says, are filled with desires brought about by sense-contact with material objects. The Buddha does not suggest we should try to remove ourselves to some place where desires do not arise; a monastery or a convent would not do, and we might seek throughout the Cosmos without ever finding such a place.

Yet such a place exists within ourselves, the Buddha taught, and finding peace calls for an abandonment of the fetter called craving. Desire is one thing – it merely arises and passes away. Craving is another – it is *clinging* to desire. It is precisely in this that suffering lies.

Attentiveness, right attention – so central is this idea to the Buddha's teaching that the 423-stanza *Dhammapada* deals with it often. The word, which means "Path of the Teaching" (*Dhamma*

= teaching + *pada* = path or way), is given to a collection of inspired verses, which are to the Buddhist scriptures what the psalms are to the Bible.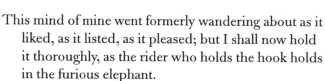

> This mind of mine went formerly wandering about as it liked, as it listed, as it pleased; but I shall now hold it thoroughly, as the rider who holds the hook holds in the furious elephant.

> If one man conquer in battle a thousand times thousand men, and if another conquer himself, he is the greatest of conquerors.

> One's own self conquered is better than all other people; not even a god, a Gandharva, nor Mara with Brahma could change into defeat the victory of a man who has vanquished himself, and always lives under restraint.

> Well-makers lead the water; fletchers bend the arrow; carpenters bend a log of wood; wise people fashion themselves.

> As a fletcher makes straight his arrow, a wise man makes straight his trembling and unsteady thought, which is difficult to keep, difficult to turn.

> As a fish taken from its watery home and thrown on the dry ground, our thought trembles all over in order to escape the domination of Mara, the tempter.

> It is good to tame the mind, which is difficult to hold in and flighty, rushing wherever it listeth; a tamed mind brings happiness.

> Let the wise man guard his thoughts, for they are difficult to perceive, very artful, and they rush wherever they list; thoughts well guarded bring happiness.

Whatever a hater may do to a hater, or an enemy to an
enemy, a wrongly-directed mind will do us greater
mischief.

Not a mother, not a father will do so much, nor any
other relative; a well-directed mind will do us
greater service.[24]

"What now," asks the Buddha, "is Right Concentration?" – the
eighth and highest step on the Noble Eightfold Path.

Fixation of the mind on a single object ("one-pointedness of
mind") is concentration.

The following, the Buddha said, are the objects of concentration or meditation: they are called the Four Fundamentals of
Attentiveness – and were mentioned earlier as attentiveness to (a)
body; (b) feeling; (c) mind, and (d) phenomena. The requisites
for concentration or meditation are the four great efforts – again,
the effort to avoid, the effort to overcome, the effort to develop,
and the effort to maintain.

How does one develop concentration or meditation? The
Buddha says that meditation is developed by practising,
developing, and cultivating these four great efforts.

Now the Buddha describes the inner states achieved by the
disciple who meditates rightly. He describes them, of course, with
authority, for he has experienced them all.

First, there is rapture and happiness, born of detachment, and
accompanied by verbal thought and rumination (pondering). This
state is achieved by the disciple who is detached from sensual
objects and from demeritorious things.

In this first state, a disciple is free of the Five Hindrances
(already given); what are present are verbal thought, rumination,
rapture, happiness, and concentration.

In the second state, even verbal thoughts and rumination fade
away, subside; the mind becomes tranquil and has achieved
"oneness"; the disciple is filled with the rapture and happiness
born of concentration.

In the third state, even rapture fades away and the disciple dwells in equanimity, is attentive, clearly conscious, and experiences a happiness born of equanimity and an attentive mind.

"And further," adds the Buddha, "after the giving up of pleasure and pain, and through the disappearance of previous joy and grief, he enters into a state beyond pleasure and pain...which is purified by equanimity and attentiveness...

"This," the Buddha concluded, "is the Middle Path ... which makes one both to see and to know, and which leads to peace, to discernment, to enlightenment, to Nirvana.

"And, following upon this path, you will put an end to suffering."

The Buddha's first sermon. Sarnath, India.
Sandstone, 5th Century CE.

Rouse thyself by thyself; examine thyself by thyself, thus
Self-protected and attentive wilt thou live happily!
The Dhammapada (v. 379)

VIII

The Ministry and Great Decease

T HE FAME OF THE FORMER Prince Siddhartha Gautama, now known as the Enlightened One, spread. Here was a young saint, people said, who spoke not only about sublime matters, but who addressed himself to all people, regardless of rank or caste, in terms that mattered to them; here was one who did not speak of gods, sacrifices, rituals or priests, but about the here-and-now, about deliverance from suffering on earth.

And how astounding were the things he taught!

He denied, for example, that there was anything permanent in us, even a soul. Everything simply "arises and passes away," he said, and the world the Buddha taught consisted merely of five groups: matter; feelings; perceptions; mental activities, and cognitions.

What are feelings and perceptions? The Buddha said they are those which arise in an individual when that person is in contact with material things. They are not permanent; they are momentary, changing, not independent. We recognise – we "see," are aware – that we have feelings and perceptions, that we feel and perceive. But, said the Buddha, that which cognises this is also momentary, changing, impermanent, not independent. Both that which sees and that which is seen are impermanent; both arise and fade away. There is *nothing*, says the Buddha, which is permanent in a human being.

This being so, the only permanent unchanging reality is to be found in Nirvana*, a "state of supreme Enlightenment beyond the conception of the intellect; the annihilation of all that we know as the personal, separative self."[25] Nirvana, explained Christmas Humphreys further, is insofar as we can understand it, "a concept of psychology, a state of consciousness." Far from committing us to "the abyss of annihilation", Buddhists see it as allowing man, through the destruction of all that is individual in him, to "enter into communion with the whole universe, and become an integral part of the great purpose."

The Buddha himself did not often use the word Nirvana; he preferred to use such expressions as not-death, release, end-of-woe, freedom, bliss, rest. "He felt that his mission was not so much to unveil the secrets of blessedness as to win men to its realisation," said one authority.[26] Yet he emphasised that Nirvana was attainable here and now, on earth, by those who had reached the goal of Buddhism, the condition of the Arhat (or, in the Pali, *Arahant*). And, because he did so, Buddhism pays most attention to the present life, not to any after-life, the very existence of which is in doubt for the Buddhist.

There were countless persons who came to the Buddha, and they arrived with endless questions. Some were troubled, confused, and genuinely searching; some merely enjoyed discussions, for philosophy has always been a favourite pastime of many in India.

They asked him about the after-life and the soul, about what happened to Buddhas themselves after death, and many other such questions. To all these, the Buddha replied that knowing the answers was not conducive to inner peace and freedom.

"Whether the Buddha lives after death or does not live after death; or whether he both lives after death and does not live after death, of only one thing may we be certain: in this life there is suffering, there is a cause of suffering, there is a cure for suffering, and there is a way which leads to the extinction of suffering."

---

* "Nirvana", as it is customarily termed, is the Sanskrit form; in the Pali, it is *Nibbana*.

The Buddha declined to answer fourteen such questions and these came to be called the Fourteen Indeterminates. Those who approached him with such speculative, "philosophical" questions, rather than to ask him how they might achieve freedom, were compared by the Buddha to a man who lay dying from a poisoned arrow.

A doctor came to draw the arrow out, but the wounded man told him to wait. First, he said, he wanted to know what kind of arrow was shot; what sort of feathers it had; who shot the arrow; what kind of person he was; what colour was his hair; what sort of poison did he use, etc.

"Such a man," said the Buddha, "would die from the poison before he could receive answers to these questions."

Life was also like that, the Buddha cautioned, and we must understand that, if answers are to be found, they will appear along the Way, and that one had best start one's journey immediately.

Often he spoke of the nature of man.* That very word deludes us into thinking that something permanent called "man" exists, says the Buddha. He again referred to the composition of "man," to the five groups which make up human beings. These he compared to the elements which make up a wagon: axle, wheels, floorboard, etc. The whole exists independently of its elements.

To those who remained perplexed, he painted another picture.

We call "river" that which is composed of countless drops of water, moving, never permanent, ever-changing. No entity called "river" truly exists; the word is merely a name we give to countless changing bubbles, drops of water, foam and waves, when these are put together.

Again, man might be compared to a candle flame, the Buddha said. This has "a sort of unity" which one can see; one calls it flame, but in actuality "flame" does not exist either permanently or independently, for the component elements which make it up change each moment, burn up, and rise again.

* Here, and throughout, obviously not meant as gender-specific

Such is man, the Buddha said. That which ties together the five groups which make up "man" is *karma* (the law of interdependent origination, often called the law of cause and effect), the merit or demerit transferred from one life to another. Yet, as to how karma operates – to this Buddha declined to reply. This, too, was one of the fourteen "indeterminates" – a profitless question, because it did not lead to enlightenment.

Always, the Buddha was intensely practical. The philosophical discussions, speculations, arguments, in which so many of his contemporaries loved to indulge were to him pointless, for was it not true that words, opinions, ideas were in themselves formless, shifting, changing, impermanent, not independent?

They too arose and faded away, mere creatures of impermanent thought. We would better occupy ourselves, he said, in pursuing the Way, in striving after enlightenment, after which the really essential truths would all be revealed to us, as indeed they had been revealed to the Buddha himself under the Bodhi-tree at Bodh-Gaya.

How foolish were those whose boat was sinking in the torrent of life and who preferred to discuss their situation rather than bail water and save themselves.

Within a short time, the fame of the Buddha had spread so widely that he amassed several thousand followers, whom he organised into a *Sangha*, or monastic Order. These monks did not live in a monastery, however, but lived together with the Buddha in temporary shelters, in parks and forests, as he travelled through the northern regions of India (now including much of Pakistan), teaching whomever he met. They joined the Sangha because they and the Buddha believed that man would more speedily reach enlightenment if he were free of worldly cares and concerns. Then he could devote himself entirely to the all-important matter of achieving his own salvation. For this reason, thousands today continue to join the Buddhist Sangha, although today the monks have largely given up wandering and preaching and have settled in permanent abodes.

In the Buddha's day, of course, the attraction of being close to the All-Enlightened One was powerful and his loving, compassionate being drew to him nobles and commoners, persons of all castes and regions. For forty-five years did the Buddha travel throughout the north of the subcontinent and his teaching spread greatly. Many of the Aryan kings were converted and granted the Buddha lands and parks where he and his followers could live in temporary camps, until the need to teach yet others would make the Buddha move once more.

The seventh member of the Buddha's order of monks (after himself and the five to whom he preached the sermon at Benares) was a wealthy young man of Benares named Yasa. He had become disgusted with his life of luxury and left the city for the deer park of Isipatana, where the Buddha was then to be found.

The Buddha taught him the Four Truths and, when Yasa's father, a gildmaster, also came to the deer park in search of his son, the Buddha instructed him in the Dhamma. The gildmaster thereupon "took his refuge" in the Buddha, the Dhamma and the Order of monks – thereby becoming the first layman to become a member of the Order under this "three-fold formula".*

Having listened to the instructions given to his father, Yasa soon attained full enlightenment, thus becoming an *arahant*, as well as the seventh member of the Sangha.‡ Significantly, the first two female lay persons to become disciples under the "three-fold" formula still in use today were Yasa's mother and his "former" wife, at whose house the Buddha accepted a meal.

The example of Yasa, who had given up his life of luxury, inspired four of his friends, all merchants' sons, to follow him into the Order; not long afterwards, fifty more of Yasa's friends joined,

---

* Tapussa and Bhallika, the merchants (and brothers) who had been the Buddha's first lay followers had of course taken "refuge" only in the Buddha and the Dhamma, for the Order had not then yet been established.

‡ The understanding of an *arahant* or *arhat* (saint) is regarded as being as great as that of the Buddha, the difference being that the Buddha obtained his understanding by his own efforts, while an *arahant* obtains it under instruction.

all becoming arahants. The Buddha is said then to have sent them out in all directions to teach the doctrine; in due course, they brought back so many would-be disciples that the Buddha was obliged to allow the monks themselves to perform the ceremony of admitting candidates into the Order. This consisted simply of removing the hair, putting on the yellow robe, and three times reciting the three-fold formula of "taking refuge in Buddha, the Doctrine and the Order".

Soon afterwards, the Buddha returned, as he had earlier promised to do, to King Bimbisara and taught him the Dhamma.

He then travelled on, teaching and "converting" many hundreds of the followers of other teachers, until his own band was numbered in the thousands. Less than a year after he had attained enlightenment, the Buddha turned his steps to Kapilavastu, his home, where he was already known as *Shakyamuni* – sage of the Shakya tribe. By this time, it is said, his followers totalled twenty thousand monks; they followed him to his home, settling themselves in the Banyan Grove outside the city. He taught his father and his cousins, including his cherished disciple, Ananda, and Devadatta, who both also joined the Sangha. Devadatta, the Buddhist "Judas", later on became a divisive element in the Order, having become jealous of and hostile to the Buddha. During this visit, it is said, some eighty thousand Sakyas, or "one per family", became followers of the Buddha.*

It was also during this visit that the Buddha had his first meeting in years with Yasodhara. As soon as she saw him, she recognised him no longer as her "husband", but as a truly different being now, a saint. He had been transformed. This she saw clearly, it is said, because of her own great piety. She called Rahula, their son, who now was a sturdy young lad, and told him to go to his father and "ask for your inheritance." The boy approached his father and made that request. The Buddha let his gaze linger on his son for a while, then turned to his chief disciple and said,

---

* It is further said that, when the Buddha was born, 80,000 Sakya families had each sworn to dedicate a son to his retinue, whether Prince Siddhartha (as he then was) became either a great religious teacher or a universal king, as had been prophesied.

"Accept the boy into the Order!" It was a spiritual inheritance the father was giving to his son, a gift he knew to be far greater than mere wealth or princely position.

The first nun in the Order is said to have been Mahaprajapati, who asked to join after the death of the Buddha's father, King Suddhodana, her husband. It was she who raised the young princeling Siddhartha after his mother died; she was his aunt, nurse, foster-mother and she had suckled him at her breast.

Three times did the widowed Mahaprajapati apply to the Buddha to enter the Order, only to be refused three times. He then travelled to Vesali, only to be followed there by his aunt and other Sakya women; they had all shaved their heads, put on the yellow robes, and repeated their request, only to be refused again three times. The disciple Ananda then intervened and asked the Buddha if a woman who had renounced her former life and assumed the doctrine and discipline of the Order were capable of Enlightenment, of *arhatship*.

"A woman is capable," said the Buddha, and told Ananda that women who took upon themselves the "eight strict Rules" could after all enter the Sangha.

These eight rules, which Mahaprajapati willingly accepted, firmly placed nuns in a distinctly inferior position to monks. Even senior nuns had to defer to novice monks, for example, nor could a nun rebuke or abuse a monk on any pretext.

The Buddha clearly remained doubtful of the wisdom of accepting women into the Order, although he presumably did not regard them as "inferior", for he had admitted to Ananda that they were as capable as men of attaining full enlightenment and becoming arahants. Having reluctantly admitted as nuns those women who accepted his eight rules, the Buddha told Ananda that their inclusion would inevitably reduce the life of the teaching from a thousand to five hundred years.

"For just as houses, where there are many women and few men, are easily broken into by robbers, even so in the doctrine and discipline in which a woman goes forth the religious system will not last long," he said. Commentators have claimed the Buddha's view of women in the Order was occasioned by his wish not to offend the prevailing customs of India; whatever his motive may have been, there are today thousands of women monks in the Order and, in countries such as Japan and Burma, they are "noted for their learning and piety," as Christmas Humphreys observed.[27]

No one in the Order was ever persuaded to enter it other than freely; for all in the Sangha, the Buddha taught a severe – if always positive and essentially hopeful – self-discipline, based on the Four Noble Truths and the Noble Eightfold Path.

"Warriors, warriors, Lord," his monks once said to him. "We call ourselves warriors. In what way are we warriors?"

"We wage war, Brethren; therefore are we called warriors."

"Wherefore, Lord, do we wage war?"

"For lofty virtue, for high endeavour, for sublime vision – for these things do we wage war. Therefore we are called warriors."[28]

But there were others who would never want to join the Sangha, who lived an ordinary life, who supported parents, wives, and children; who were in business, or worked the land, or ruled people. What could the Buddha teach them? How might those order their life who wished to follow the teaching without joining the Order?

This question was put to the Buddha one day by a young man named Singala, the son of a local householder, at a time when the Buddha was staying in the bamboo grove at Rajagaha.

"Listen," the Buddha told Singala, "and I'll tell you. Mark well what I say!"

The noble lay disciple, he said, gives up four vices of action, does no evil deed from the four motives, avoids the six ways of squandering his wealth, and avoids all fourteen evils. In doing so, he is ready for the conquest of both worlds, is fortunate both in this world and the next.

"What are the four vices of action that he gives up? They are injury to life, stealing, base conduct in sexual matters, and false speech.

"What are the four motives of evil deeds which he avoids? Evil deeds are committed from partiality, enmity, stupidity, and fear.

"And what are the six ways of squandering wealth? They are addiction to drink, which is the cause of carelessness; roaming the streets at improper times; frequenting fairs and other public amusements; gambling; keeping bad company, and idleness.

"There are six dangers in addiction to drink: one may actually lose one's health; one is more likely to quarrel; one is liable to illness; one's reputation is lowered; one is likely to act foolish and indecent; and one weakens one's intelligence.

"There are six dangers in roaming in the street at improper times: the man who does so is unprotected and unguarded; so are his wife and family, with whom he ought to be; likewise his property is unguarded; he looks suspicious to others; he is the subject of false rumours; in fact, he meets with all kinds of troubles which he would not encounter if he remained where he ought to be.

"There are six dangers in frequenting places of public amusements: the man who does so cannot do without dancing, singing, music, story-telling, jugglers and acrobats; in fact he becomes addicted to amusements.

"There are six dangers in gambling: the winner is hated; the loser regrets the loss of his money; there is obvious loss of wealth; a gambler's word is not respected in courts of law; he is scorned by friends and counsellors, and he is not cultivated by decent people who wish to find husbands for their daughters, for a gambler who is always dicing isn't fit to keep a wife.

"There are six dangers in idleness: a man says 'it's too cold' and doesn't work; or he says 'it's too hot'; or 'it's too early'; or 'it's too late'; or 'I'm too hungry'; or 'I'm too full'. And so all this time he won't do what he ought to do, earns no new wealth, but fritters away that which he has already earned.

"There are four types of men who should be looked upon as enemies who disguise themselves as friends: a grasping man; a smooth-spoken man; a man who only says what you want to hear, and a man who helps you waste your money.

"The grasping man is an enemy because he is grasping, because he expects a lot in return whenever he gives a little, because he performs duty only out of fear, and because he only serves his own interests.

"The smooth-spoken man is an enemy because he says only soothing things to you about the past and about the future, because he tries to win you over with empty promises, and because he shows his shortcomings whenever there's anything to be done.

"The man who says only what you like to hear is an enemy because he consents to an evil deed and doesn't consent to a good one, because he praises you to your face, but runs you down behind your back.

"The wastrel is an enemy because he is your companion when you drink, when you roam the streets at improper times, when you go to amusements, and when you gamble.

"Yet there are four types who should be looked upon as true friends: a man who wants to help you; a man who is a friend in good and bad weather; a man who gives good advice; and a man who is sympathetic."

Having told the young Singala whom to avoid and whom to cultivate, the Buddha now addressed himself to the question of how a lay disciple should behave to his parents, his teachers, his wife and children, his friends and counsellors, his servants, and holy men – and what kind of behaviour he might expect from them in return.

In this discourse, the Buddha teaches an ethic which retains its force and relevance today and which would most probably be acceptable to modern men and women, of whatever religious persuasion they may be. Even agnostics could accept it, so long as they are not too much persuaded by modern fashion that the emphasis should be put onto "human rights", rather than "duties".

The Buddha said:

"A son should serve his mother and father in this way: having been maintained by them in his childhood, he should maintain them in their old age; he should perform the duties which formerly were theirs; he should maintain the honour and traditions of his family; he should make himself worthy of his heritage, and he should venerate deceased family members.

"Father and mother should in turn serve their son in the following way: they should restrain him from evil, encourage him to do good, have him taught a profession, see to it that he is married to a suitable wife, and transfer his inheritance to him in due time.

"A pupil should serve his teacher in these ways: he should rise respectfully when he enters; he should wait upon him; he should be willing to learn; he should serve him attentively, and he should be diligent about his studies.

"The teacher in turn should serve his pupil in these ways: he should train him to conduct himself well; he should teach him so that he remembers what he has been taught; he should instruct him thoroughly; he should speak well of him to others, and he should protect him in all ways.

"A husband should serve his wife by honouring her, by respecting her, by remaining faithful to her, by putting her in charge of his home, and by duly giving her adornments.

"And the wife, in turn, should serve her husband by being efficient at home, by managing servants well, by being chaste, by taking care of the goods he brings home, and by being skilful and untiring in her duties.

"A gentlemen serves his friends and counsellors in these ways: by being generous and courteous towards them, by helping them, by treating them as he would treat himself, and by keeping his word to them.

"They, in turn, should serve him by protecting him when he is careless, by guarding his property on such occasions, by being a refuge for him when he is in trouble, by remaining loyal to him in misfortune, and by respecting members of his family.

"A master serves his servants in these ways: by assigning work to them in proportion to their strength, by giving them due food and wages, by caring for them in sickness, by sharing luxuries with them, and by giving them appropriate holidays.

"They, in turn, serve their master properly by getting up before he does and by going to bed after he does; by being content with what he gives them; by doing their work well, and by talking well about him to others.

118

"A gentleman serves holy men in these ways: by affectionate acts, words, and thoughts; by opening his door to them, and by providing them with food. They in turn serve him by restraining him from evil and encouraging him to do good, by feeling for him with a friendly mind, by teaching him things he did not know before, by encouraging him to follow what he has already learned, and by showing him the way to spiritual development."

The foregoing discourse of the Buddha is only one of a vast number, for the Buddha spent more than four fruitful decades teaching. He opened the eyes of most of those who came to him, clarified his teaching endlessly, until today there remains an unprecedented, rich legacy of instructive and inspirational stories about him. Too many to be retold here, they include tales of treachery and opposition to the Buddha, both from rival teachers and from his jealous cousin, the monk Devadatta, who even tried to have the Buddha killed.

This occurred thirty-seven years after the Buddha's enlightenment. Devadatta first tried to take over the Order, citing the Buddha's advanced age; failing at that, he tried to have him assassinated, a plan which backfired when the two hired assassins were so affected by seeing the Buddha that they became his disciples. Devadatta then tried to stage an accident, but the rock that rolled down a mountain and was to have killed the Buddha merely caused a scratch. Devadatta's final attempt involved a maddened elephant, but this beast succumbed to the Buddha's calm benevolence towards it, and knelt at his feet, cured of its mad rage. Eventually, Devadatta died, though not before having sown the seeds of a schism within the Order, traces of which lasted for several centuries.[29]

Here, in this narrative, we do not have space to include more of such stories than the essentials. We have pointed to the core of the teaching, the Four Noble Truths and the Noble Eightfold Path, and given examples of what the Buddha had to say to his contemporaries – and to us – about how one might order one's life and live it, to come to the inner freedom of which the Buddha taught. Words and books can take a man only so far in the Dhamma, for it is no accident that it is called a Way and Path. Buddhism, like other great traditional teachings, is a psychological as well as spiritual journey for which the Buddha provides the directions. It is, put simply, about how human beings may through their own efforts work to transform themselves. The Buddha never demands; he proposes. The Buddhist can but try to follow the Path faithfully.

The Western student, noted Humphreys, must understand that the Buddhist does not take a solemn oath, when he undertakes to renounce attachment to a particular demeritorious way of conduct. Such an undertaking "is not a vow to God or any other Being, but a solemn undertaking to oneself". Nor is it even an undertaking "never to kill or lie as the case may be, but a vow... to train oneself to diminish one's attachment to the error specified. For Buddhism is at all times a reasonable Middle Way, and all that a man may usefully undertake is to wean himself with diligence from the ways of darkness (personal desire) and to set himself in the Way of light."[30]

The story of the Buddha's own journey ends with the termination of his life, called by the Buddhists the Sutta (*Discourse, or Sermon*) of the Great Decease.

The Buddha was now nearly 80 years old and ill. Thousands of his monks were staying with him outside Vaisali in a grove of sal trees, grieving at his impending death. The Buddha knew well that he was dying but, for a time, put down his disease so that he could continue to teach for a while longer. Then, finally, when he felt the time was appropriate, he asked Ananda, his chief disciple, to prepare a couch for him. "I am weary," he said, "and wish to lie down." Ananda asked the dying Buddha, now surrounded by his monks, what instructions he might leave for the Sangha, the Order.

"What!" the Buddha exclaimed. "Do you expect that from me? If there is anyone here who is thinking now, 'I shall lead the Order' or 'the Order depends on me,' let such a man make up instructions. The Buddha does not think this way, so how can he leave instructions?"

In his last days, the Buddha was asked about women by Ananda. "How are we to conduct ourselves, Lord, with regard to womankind?"

"Don't see them, Ananda," the Buddha replied.

"But if we should see them, what are we to do?"

"Abstain from speech, Ananda."

"But if they should speak to us, Lord, what are we to do?"

"Keep wide awake, Ananda."

To those who bemoaned his passing, the Buddha emphasised again, "How could it be otherwise? Have I not told you that decay is inherent in all component things?" His last moments were devoted to re-emphasising the need to start on the journey now, that there was little time to waste, and that a man who is energetic in his pursuit of this goal shall find it.

"Be your own lamps, your own refuge!" he told the assembled monks. "Seek refuge in nothing but yourselves! Hold to the truth as to a lamp and a refuge and do not look for refuge outside yourselves!

"A monk," he continued, "becomes his own refuge by constantly watching over his body, feelings, perceptions, mental formations, and states of consciousness in such a way that he overcomes the cravings and depressions of ordinary men, so that he is always strenuous, self-possessed, and collected in mind. Whichever among you does this, either now or after I am dead, if he is anxious to learn, he shall reach the summit!"

And then, just before closing his eyes, the Buddha looked about him again. "Decay is inherent in all component things!" he said. "Work out your salvation with diligence!"

Thereafter, he closed his eyes and, it is said, passed through the various stages of consciousness which only the All-Enlightened One can know, ended his last incarnation on earth, and passed from sight.

Years later, a Buddhist sage was asked by an Indian king whether the Buddha still existed.

"He does, Lord!" the sage replied.

"But where?" asked the king.

The monk answered that the Lord Buddha had passed to complete Nirvana and could not be pointed out. There was nothing left which could lead to the formation of another being.

"What do you mean?" asked the king.

"This is an illustration," answered the sage. "Supposing we saw a great fire, could we point out in it an individual flame which had gone out and say it is here or there?"

"No," said the king. "For the flame has gone out and its elements cannot be found."

"This is just how the Lord Buddha has gone into Nirvana," said the monk. "We can detect him only in his Teaching, for it was he who taught it."

The Buddha Teaching. Gandhara, Afghanistan.
Stone, 2nd or 3rd Century CE.

The thoughtless man, even if he can recite a large
portion of the Law, but is not a doer of it, has no
share in the priesthood, but is like a cowherd
counting the cows of others.

The Dhammapada (v. 19)

IX

The Life of the Teaching

BUDDHISM IS TODAY MORE THAN 2,500 years old – and this fact
alone makes it clear that it must have undergone a great
historical development and many changes since the Buddha's
decease. Historical events alone have had a profound effect on this
teaching, for the history of more than two millennia is crowded
with countless such events, which we cannot chronicle here. This
narrative, moreover, is about the Buddha and his teaching more
than it is about his Sangha, his converts, or the nations which have
adopted his faith.

During those 2,500 years, Buddhism, like all other spiritual
teachings, met with fierce and even deadly resistance in some
places, and with a heartfelt welcome in others.

What general statements may be made about the growth of
Buddhism? One which stands out as a noble and unique fact is
this: in all the years of its existence, Buddhism has never shed
blood in the Buddha's name! This is remarkable indeed, consid-
ering the nature of man, the historical events which Buddhism met
during these 2,500 years, and the example of religious hatred and
intolerance given by other members of the human race! More than
anything else, it shows us the force of the Buddha's compassionate
doctrine and shows us again that, for Buddhists, this teaching is a
way of life and a way of living, rather than an abstract "faith"
which belongs mainly in the temple. The Buddha taught that man

must transform himself; Buddhism's history shows us that this has had its meaning for even the humblest adherent.

Buddhism is essentially an ethic; some have gone so far as to call it the world's only "atheist" or "agnostic" religion; certainly the Buddha never promised a man rewards in any afterlife. There are few observances and the teaching is loosely-knit, for there is no central Buddhist authority. Each Buddhist church or temple is independent – joined together only by a common adherence to the "Four Words" and the Noble Eightfold Path. And, as has been said, even these are not final authorities, for they serve the Buddhist only as guides.

The factor which caused Buddhism to grow so greatly since the Buddha's death is, perhaps more than any other, the vitality of the Buddhist Sangha. Unique among other religious teachings, it was established directly by the Founder himself, in that he himself collected thousands of monks and nuns about him, giving them a mission: to preach.

Not to convert, but just to preach. Again, Buddhism's 2,500 years show us no evidence of anyone ever having been converted forcibly or in any way against their will. Always the monks seem to have followed the Buddha's injunction to speak "moderately and full of sense"; those who rejected the Dhamma went on their way with a blessing from the bhikkhu who had tried to teach them, for the Buddha emphasised that no man may stand in another's way towards his own salvation. And so Buddhism "converted" only those who welcomed it; in a sense, each individual has had to make his own personal decision regarding the Dhamma, after a personal evaluation of its central message. And because nothing in the teaching must be taken on faith, that which is accepted by the individual Buddhist is reasonable to his mind and thus commands his allegiance.

The Sangha presented the message of the Buddha to many lands in Asia and the following were converted to Buddhism: Ceylon (Sri Lanka today), Burma, Siam (Thailand today), Cambodia, China, Korea, Japan, and Tibet. In each it tended to take slightly different forms and the Buddhism of some of these nations varies greatly

from that of others. Yet common principles underlie them all: the
Four Noble Truths and the Noble Eightfold Path.

A few hundred years after the Buddha's death, Buddhism split
into two main schools: the Theravada – orthodox, guardians of
the original message of the Dhamma, the name meaning "doctrine
of the elders", and the Mahayana, meaning "Greater Vehicle of the
Truth" – intellectual, mystical, boldly speculative.

Theravadists regard the Mahayanists as more or less in error,
as having departed from the sublimity of the rigorous teaching of
old, even as having "corrupted" Buddhism; the Mahayanists, on
the other hand, regard the "old believers" as merely limited in
their viewpoint, teaching the true Dhamma as far as it goes, but
unwilling to take bold steps towards a greater exploration of the
Buddha's meaning. Because many of the Southeast Asian countries are largely Theravadist, this branch of Buddhism has come to
be called the "Southern School"; because China, Korea, Japan
and Tibet have largely followed Mahayanist thought, this school
has come to be called the "Northern School".

There seems to be little disagreement about the Theravadist
statement that they teach "the ancient doctrine". It is considered
to be more difficult, more strict, than is that taught by the
Mahayana. It has tolerated few speculations, few mystical flights,
few metaphysical innovations or interpretations. Its adherents
concentrate upon the original Dhamma and its very rigidity is
regarded by the Theravadists as proof of its faithfulness to the early
message of the Buddha, while Mahayanists regard that rigidity as
a limitation.

For the Mahayana School has encouraged individual exploration, a fact which has caused the birth of a host of Mahayanist
schools, from Zen in China, Korea and Japan to Tantric and
Lamaist Buddhism in Tibet. It has accommodated itself to the
prevailing customs and beliefs of the lands it has entered and
adopted many aspects of religions other than Buddhism in the
process.

It was shortly after the death of the Buddha that the monk Mahakassapa, with a great number of fellow-bhikkhus, retired to Rajagaha under the patronage of the ruler Ajatasattu to convene what has come to be known as the First Buddhist Council. The Buddha had given countless discourses during his 45-year ministry; it now seemed appropriate to review them and to compile them in an orderly manner, into what were called *Pitakas* – "baskets" holding the teaching. None of them had ever been written down; monks had memorised them as they were given, had passed them on orally, in the Indian tradition.

The monk Upali spoke for the *Vinaya-pitaka*, the message of the Buddha regarding his Order, the Sangha. Ananda, the Buddha's chief disciple, spoke for the Dhamma itself, while Mahakassapa posed them both questions. In addition to the *Vinaya-pitaka*, two other "baskets" resulted from this Council, the *Sutta-pitaka*, comprising the Buddha's discourses, and the *Abhidhamma-pitaka*, his more psychological and philosophical message.

The Council was held in democratic fashion and the method used was "dialectical", points being raised through logical disputation. We may be sure that the monks who gathered round listened carefully, for they would soon be called upon to recite these Pitakas to those who were eager to hear Buddha's message. And, even today, each tale about Gautama Buddha begins in the same way, with the words, "Thus have I heard" – in token of this oral teaching.

It was slightly more than a hundred years later (383 BCE) that the Second Council met at Vesali. Much had happened in India during those years. The government succeeding Ajatasattu became corrupt, developed into "a dynasty of parricides". This was overthrown by the people, who put into power a minister named Susunaga. It was during the reign of his son Kalasoka that the Second Council met.

But the years had not only brought political ferment. It was at this council that the first signs of a rift in Buddhism appeared. The council began with a disputation about ten of the Buddha's restrictions for monks; two of these dealt with drinking unfermented palm wine and accepting gold and silver. This dispute caused intrigue, until finally the split burst into the open. The monk Revata presided over several hundred bhikkhus who upheld the ten restrictions, but others predictably wished to relax rules they considered irksome. These formed themselves into a group called the Mahasangiti.

Once unity is broken, it is easy for complete fragmentation to begin. This is precisely what happened. From the rebellious Mahasangiti there sprang five additional factions, while even the orthodox split into twelve sects. Years later, around 247 BCE, all were to be declared heretical except one of the orthodox schools. What finally developed is that this school came to be the Theravadist one, while the Mahasangiti gradually developed into the Mahayana school.

It was during the reign of the Emperor Asoka that this latter development took place.

His reign is referred to as a Golden Age, which brought India together, for a short time, into an united, happy, prosperous Buddhist nation. Asoka was a warrior, the grandson of the great Chandragupta who had defeated the armies of Alexander the Great, after the Macedonian's death. Asoka himself had fought many battles and his last was particularly bloody. According to his own reckoning, his victory was won at the expense of 100,000 killed in battle, 150,000 captured, and in many times that number wounded.

He turned from that battlefield of carnage in horror and revulsion. Although he had emerged the victor, he was disgusted with war and slaughter. Although a great warrior, he realised the futility of war, the misery it causes, and the evil of causing suffering. And so Asoka was won over to the doctrine of Buddha and embraced the Buddhist concept of *ahimsa*, non-violence to living beings.

Asoka was an absolute but benevolent ruler. He improved his people's lot both spiritually and materially, setting the tone for a generally high morality and exemplifying in his own life all the

Buddhist virtues of compassion, selflessness, and dedication to the general good. Asoka himself even joined the Sangha, as did his son and daughter.

It was he who convened the Third Buddhist Council in the seventeenth year of his reign (252 BCE) and, at its end, he ordered missionaries to be sent to the inhabitants of his empire, to the border nations, the forest tribes, the southern kingdoms including Ceylon and, according to some accounts, even to the Greek states and the Malayan Archipelago.

It was Asoka's son, the bhikkhu Mahinda, who brought Buddhism to what is called Sri Lanka today, the island of Ceylon, which lies off the south-east coast of India, in the Indian Ocean. He did so at the invitation of Ceylon's king, Tissa, who became a fervent adherent of the Theravada School. Mahinda's sister, Sanghamitta, followed her brother to the island, bringing with her a cutting of the original Bodhi-tree under which Gautama found enlightenment. Today, within the ruins of the ancient capital of Ceylon, Anuradhapura, there stands an enormous pipal tree, reputedly the 2,000 years old outgrowth of this cutting. Ceylon was also presented with other objects of Buddhist veneration – two relics of the Buddha himself, a collarbone and a tooth – and great temples were built to house these. Yet more important is another expenditure of Ceylonese energy, for the Buddhists of that island were the first to write down the entire Buddhist Canon, the Pitakas, around the first century BCE. Also, they produced a Buddhist commentator, Buddhagosa, who around 500 CE formalised the Theravada teaching in his great work, *Visuddhimagga*, the "path to Purity". Even today, the beautiful island of Sri Lanka is venerated by Buddhists the world over as the unofficial centre of Theravada Buddhism and as a place where the Dhamma took root firmly, bearing abundant fruit.

Many political events were to affect Buddhism during the first century of the Christian Era. Scythians from Chinese Turkestan swept into north-western India and Kaniska, one of the Scythian rulers in India, became a great Buddhist patron. The Greeks also re-asserted themselves and one of their rulers, Menander, became a patron of Buddhism.

Kaniska convened the Fourth Buddhist Council in India, during the very time that the entirely separate Fourth Council (the one at which the Pitakas were written down) met in Ceylon. The Indian council is important also, for it resulted in the rise of the Mahayana School and because it was during this period that Buddhism made its first contact with Chinese-speaking people.

In China itself, the Han dynasty (206 BCE—220 CE) had consolidated its empire under the laws of Confucius, but these soon broke down, creating a vacuum into which Taoism moved, along with Buddhism. Taoism is a Chinese teaching with many similarities to the teaching of the Buddha and their adherents apparently co-operated. Gradually, Buddhism gained strength in China, though its experience there depended overly much on whether the ruler of the day happened to be a Buddhist or a Confucian. Monasteries were, however, established and, over the centuries, Buddhism, together with Taoism and Confucianism, became important in China. It was there that Zen took root.

As time passed, Buddhism gradually died out in India itself, until today only a tiny fraction of its population is Buddhist. The reasons are both political and religious, but it is enough to say that, as Buddhism gained strength elsewhere, it lost it in the land of the Buddha, where Brahmanism re-established itself strongly. Today, you will find the Buddha claimed by the Hindus as one of the Hindu deities and his statue today even presides over many a Brahman ritual.

Buddhism firmly implanted itself in Southeast Asia, bringing with it a flowering of art and culture. In Burma, to cite one example, it brought a flowering of architecture at a time – approximately 1050 CE – when Europeans were just moving out of the Dark Ages and into the Mediaeval period. In Pagan, the ancient Burmese capital, for example, thousands of temples called pagodas were built within a mere few square miles and Rangoon, today's capital, contains the startlingly beautiful Shwe Dagon pagoda, 368 feet high and covered completely in gold. This structure is as high as a thirty-storey skyscraper – yet it was built almost a thousand years ago.

To the North, in China, the special school of Buddhism called Zen was developing. In 250 CE, the Indian Buddhist sage Bodhi-Dharma brought with him the four-line message which is the central, mystifying, and subtle core of Zen:

> "A special transmission outside the scriptures;
> No dependence upon words and letters;
> Direct pointing at the soul of man;
> Seeing into one's nature and the attainment of
> Buddhahood."

Adherents of this teaching go back beyond Bodhi-Dharma to explain the origin of Zen. One day, they say, the Buddha himself sat on the mount of the Holy Vulture, teaching his monks. This time, however, he chose not to provide them with a sermon, but instead picked up a bouquet of flowers someone had given him as a gift, and held it aloft for his monks to see. He did so without comment.

All except one – the venerable Mahakassapa – were mystified. Mahakassapa quietly smiled, whereupon the Buddha, seeing that he had understood, turned to him and said, "I have the most precious treasure, spiritual and transcendental, which at this moment I turn over to you!"

Direct knowledge of the Law, without books or formal teaching, but through seeing into one's own inner nature – this is what Bodhi-Dharma taught. Many are the tales of his life and work in China, for he is said to have lived to the extraordinary age of one hundred and fifty years – if, indeed, he lived at all, for some regard him as a mythical character.

Shortly after Buddhism had implanted itself in China, it travelled to Korea. Today, that land remains a stronghold of Zen, with many Buddhist monasteries, but historically, Korea's importance to Buddhism lies in that it opened up the road to Japan.

It entered the Japanese islands in 552 CE and within a few years found in the Regent Shotoku Taishi a great patron who was to become a Buddhist scholar of note. It was in Japan that Zen was to reach its final development. The word Zen is itself a corruption of the Chinese word Ch'an, in itself a corruption of the Indian Dhyana.

In the meantime, Buddhism had developed still differently in that mysterious "land of peaks and lamas" – Tibet.

Tibet has always attracted the interest of Western man, if only because of its mystery and inaccessibility. Hidden in the remotest parts of the Himalayan range, due north of India and west of China, it is reachable only via tortuous mountain passes and was virtually unknown until a half century or so ago, when Westerners first began to penetrate it.

For a long time, Tibet remained the Forbidden Land, which permitted no foreigners to enter. What were the Tibetans protecting so jealously? Perhaps many things, but certainly they were protecting their way of life, protecting themselves from "modernisation" and "Westernisation", those tendencies which, while they brought benefits to many peoples, have also destroyed much of great traditional value. The Tibetans revered their way of life and wanted to be left alone to follow it. A cruel fate has since placed them under the barbaric rule of Communist China.

Tibet had traditionally been ruled by monks and priests and the life of the Tibetan people had been oriented towards the Buddhist Dhamma. Indeed, vast numbers of the male population were monks and the supreme ruler of the nation, His Holiness the Dalai Lama, is even in exile a force to be reckoned with in the entire Buddhist world.

Tibetan Buddhism is extremely complex and intermixed with a host of other beliefs, especially an earlier Tibetan teaching called Bön and a form of Indian Buddhism called Tantric Buddhism. This latter teaching has strong "esoteric" elements, meaning it is passed on orally to trained disciples and select initiates. The Buddha himself rejected esotericism and stated he kept nothing back to teach only to a group of developed people.

We refer to Tibetan Buddhism generally as "Lamaism", but that words signifies a teaching followed by the majority of the

Tibetan priesthood. It countenances many things which may seem strange to us after we have studied the Buddha's life: worship, rites, prayers, the idea of intercession, and other forms of the devotional life.

How could this be, when the Buddha himself deplored dependence on gods?

The answer lies in the Mahayanan deification of what is called "the Buddha-principle". Gautama was a man, they said, but in achieving Buddhahood, he became a god. And since Gautama Buddha himself admitted that he was the fifth of a line of incarnated Buddhas, then it follows that there are five gods to worship. Not only were there five, however, but a veritable host, for the Mahayanists believe that Buddhahood lies latent in each man and that many have reached the stage of enlightenment, thus also becoming divine in the Buddha-essence. It is their Buddhahood, not they themselves, which is worshipped. Still, inevitably, prayers and temples and rites were established.

The Mahayanists took one further step and held out the possibility of intercession. A man who believes firmly enough in the Dhamma and who prays fervently enough to the Buddhas can achieve merit, they stated. Of course, this is disputed by the old believers, the Theravadists.

Such theological disputes are not terribly meaningful to the average Buddhist, nor perhaps even to many Buddhist monks. Within the past century, they have signified their agreement to a number of basic Buddhist principles, most of them the ones raised in this book. In 1891, an American, Colonel H. S. Olcott, founding president of the Theosophical Society, formulated fourteen Fundamental Buddhist Beliefs, and in the 1940's, Christmas Humphreys of the Buddhist Society in London put together his Principles of Buddhism. Adherents of all schools signified agreement with these points, put down by an American and an Englishman.

Yet this is not strange to the Buddhist, for he would regard the teaching of the Lord Buddha as universal and as having meaning to many in many lands. In recent times, there has grown in the

West a great new interest in Buddhism and the Japanese form of Zen has particularly attracted Westerners. Since the collapse of communism, interest in Buddhism has also grown in Eastern Europe, including Russia.*

While the Occidental world's knowledge of the Dhamma is hardly more than a hundred and fifty years old and therefore relatively new, it is probable that more and more Occidentals will be prompted to study the words of Gautama Buddha. They may not thereby become Buddhists, but in broadening their own appreciation of the wisdom of the East, they will benefit from tasting the Buddha's sublime and compassionate Way of self-development.

Other "Ways" exist, and it is up to each searching man or woman to find – and follow – that path which best speaks to them. Whichever they follow, however, it is likely they will encounter in it these universal Buddhist truths:

"Cease to do evil, learn to do good, cleanse your own heart; this is the Teaching..."[31]

* For this, and Buddhism's encounter with Western culture in general, see Stephen Batchelor's *The Awakening of the West* (London: HarperCollins Aquarian imprint, 1994).

Appendices

Source Notes

Where appropriate, occasional sources are listed numerically in footnotes within the text; other important sources, especially of the Buddha's own words, as in Pali texts (*Digha-Nikaya, Majjhima-Nikaya, Anguttara-Nikaya, Samyutta-Nikaya, Sutta-Nipata, Udana, Dhammapada and Itivuttaka*), may be found in a variety of translations, as for example in the following:

Selections from various Pali scriptures, as given in A *Buddhist Bible*, revised & enlarged edition, edited by Dwight Goddard (New York: E. P. Dutton & Co., Inc., 1938), specifically from *The Word of the Buddha*, a selection made by the Venerable Bhikkhu Nyanatiloka, a German Buddhist abbot in Ceylon, originally published in a pamphlet dated 1935. Also, Bhikkhu Nyanatiloka, *The Word of the Buddha*, as given in *Buddha: Life & Teachings*, with illustrations by Jeanyee Wong (Mt. Vernon, New York: Peter Pauper Press, no date given). Also, as given in *The Vedantic Buddhism of the Buddha*, specifically *Part I: The Buddha and the Dhamma*, translated from the original Pali and edited by J. G. Jennings (London: Oxford University Press, 1948). Also, Edward Conze and others (editors), *Buddhist Texts Through the Ages* (New York: Harper & Row Harper Torchbooks, 1964).

See also Bibliography for other works to which I am indebted.

Notes on spellings

The spelling of individuals' proper names, as of place-names, titles, etc., varies in scholarly reference works and Buddhist scriptures. In general, this text adheres to spellings customary in translations from Pali texts (Dhamma, for example, instead of the Sanskrit "Dharma") but I am conscious of being inconsistent whenever the reader may be assumed to be more familiar with the later Sanskrit rendering, rather than the earlier Pali. Thus, for example, while the Pali "Gotama" is often used instead of the Sanskrit Gautama, I have chosen the Sanskrit form; it also explains, for example, why Nirvana (Sanskrit) is used instead of the more unfamiliar Pali "Nibbana". As for diacritical signs, these have deliberately been omitted throughout the text.

Chronology

563 BCE	Birth of Prince Siddhartha Gautama, the future Buddha
534 BCE	Prince Siddhartha's "Great Renunciation", at age 29
528 BCE	Buddha's Enlightenment, at age 35
483 BCE	Buddha's death, at age 80

Notes

1. Christmas Humphreys, *Buddhism* (London: Penguin Books, 1951), page 26.
2. Irving Babbitt, "Buddha and the Occident", in *The Dhammapada* (N.Y.: Oxford University Press, 1936; New Directions paperback, 1965), page 110.
3. Sir Edwin Arnold, *The Light of Asia, or The Great Renunciation* (New York, A. L. Burt Co., 1879).
4. From the Buddhist Canon (*Anguttara-nikaya*), as given in Edward J. Thomas, *The Life of Buddha as Legend and History*, (London: Routledge and Kegan Paul, 1927; paperback 1975) page 47.
5. Arnold, *op.cit.*, p. 8.
6. *Ibid.*
7. Arnold, *op. cit.*, p. 21.
8 In the midst of 84,000 women attendants, according to certain Buddhist scriptures.
9. Arnold, *op. cit.*, p. 43.
10. Thomas, *op. cit.*, p. 54.
11. *Ibid.*
12. Humphreys, *Exploring Buddhism*, (London: George Allen & Unwin Ltd., 1974) page 52.
13. *Majjhima Nikaya* (Pali Text Society translation: "Middle Length Sayings"), as given in H. W. Schumann, *The Historical Buddha* (London: Penguin Arkana, 1989), page 52.
14. As quoted in Thomas, *op. cit.*, page 71.
15. Jean Boisselier, in *The Wisdom of the Buddha* (London: Thames and Hudson, 1994) page 56.
16. From *Majjhima Nikaya* (Pali translation "Middle Length Sayings"), as quoted by H. W. Schumann, *The Historical Buddha* (Penguin Arkana, 1989) pages 55–56.
17. As given in Boisselier, *op. cit.*, pages 72–73.

18. T. W. Rhys Davids, *Buddhist Suttas*, of which he was translator from the Pali (New York: Dover Publications Inc., 1969) pages 142–43. Republished from Vol. XI of *The Sacred Books of the East*, first published 1881 by Clarendon Press, Oxford.

19. Humphreys, *Buddhism, op. cit.*, page 81.

20. Humphreys, *Buddhism, op. cit.*, page 111.

21. Quoted by P. Laksmi Narasu, *The Essence of Buddhism*, as cited by Humphreys, *Buddhism, op. cit.*, page 112.

22. *Christian Yoga* by J.-M. Dechanet, O.S.B. (New York and London 1960; Paris 1956). At the time of writing his book, Father Dechanet, a monk of the Benedictine Abbey of Saint-André, was prior of the Monastery of Saint-Benoit. He had for some time been training monks under his direction in techniques of Yoga, which he considers of great value in the Christian and, particularly, monastic life.

23. A. R. Orage, *The Active Mind: Adventures in Awareness* (New York: Hermitage House, 1954), p. 20.

24. *The Dhammapada*, translated from the Pali by F. Max Mueller (Chicago: Rajput Press 1911), verses 33–6; 42; 43; 80; 103; 104; 326. See also Irving Babbitt, *The Dhammapada* (N.Y.: Oxford University Press, 1936; New Directions Paperback, 1965).

25. Humphreys, *Buddhism, op. cit.*, page 244.

26. Professor Radhakrishnan, in *Indian Philosophy*, Vol. I (*Gautama the Buddha*), page 447, as quoted by Humphreys, *op. cit.*, page 127.

27. Humphreys, *Buddhism, op. cit.*, page 141.

28. *Anguttara Nikaya*, as quoted in Humphreys, *ibid.*, page 129.

29. Boisselier, *op cit,* pages 95–97.

30. Humphreys, *Buddhism, op.cit.*, page 240.

31. As given in Humphreys, *Buddhism, op. cit.*, page 75.

Glossary

Ahimsa Buddhist doctrine of non-violence, gentleness to all forms of life.

Alara Kalapa Brahmanic sage and guru, one of Gautama's teachers.

Ananda Name of the Buddha's personal attendant and beloved disciple. In Hindu, Ananda means "joy" and is used as suffix to the names of many Hindu teachers.

Anata "He Who Has Understood". Title given to Kondanna (*q.v.*).

Anatta The denial of the Hindu concept of Atman (*q.v.*). Along with Anicca (*q.v.*) and Dukkha, one of the three "Signs of Being".

Anicca Impermanence, change. Along with Anatta (*q.v.*) and Dukkha (*q.v.*), one of the three "Signs of Being".

Arahant, or **Arhat** One who through the Buddha's Way has become enlightened and attained Nirvana. A saint.

Ardjuna One of Prince Siddhartha's rivals for hand of Yasodhara.

Arhat Sanskrit spelling of the Pali *Arahant* (*q.v.*).

Aruparaga Demon unleashed by Mara (*q.v.*), representing "Lust of Fame".

Aryans, or **Aryas** Name of people migrating into and populating Indian subcontinent approx. 1500 BCE. Word means "noblemen" or "owners of land".

Asita "Great Sage", who is said to have transported himself from the Himalayas to King Suddhodhana's court, to worship the future Buddha after his birth. (Compare Wise Men of Christian legend.)

Asoka Indian king-emperor (d. *circa* 237 BCE; reigned *c.*255—*c.*237 BCE), converted to Buddhism c.257 BCE.

Atman Brahmanist concept of the breath as an immortal soul, the self or ego. In some old Brahman schools, it constitutes a metaphysical being in man, denial of which (*Anatta*) is part of the Buddha's teaching.

Attavada Demon unleashed by Mara (*q.v.*), representing Egoism, "Sin of Self".

Bhagavad Gita Religious poem of Brahamism and Hinduism.

Bhallika Name of one of two merchants who became the Buddha's first lay followers.

Bhikkhu A Buddhist monk, mendicant, friar. Today, specifically a monk of Theravada school. (Sanskrit: Bhikshu.)

Boddhisattva "Awakening being", one who aspires to become a Buddha; a saint, about to become a Buddha. In later Buddhism, any religious teacher or preacher.

Bimbisara King and early convert of the Buddha.

Bo-tree Wild fig tree (*ficus religiosa*), a pipal, beneath which Gautama attained to Buddhahood. Bodhi-tree, as it is also called, means Tree of Enlightenment.

Bodh-Gaya Site of original Bodhi-tree.

Bodhi-Dharma Indian Buddhist sage (*c.*250 CE), said to have brought to China the message which resulted in Zen school. Said to have for 150 years, but is possibly mythical.

Bön Indigenous, animist religion of Tibet.

Boustrophedon A system of writing used in early Indian subcontinent.

Brahma Sanskrit for ultimate, absolute, universal Force, "God" in its most abstract form; creator of the Universe.

Brahman Member of highest, priestly caste, though not necessarily priests, as members of this caste were often high officials serving kings, or merchants or farmers.

Brahmanas Commentaries in the Vedas (*q.v.*).

Brahmanism Indian religion based on Brahmanas, Vedas (*q.v.*), precurser of Hinduism (*q.v.*).

Buddha Literally, the Awakened One, or the Enlightened One, derived from root *budh*, "to know".

Buddhagosa Buddhist author (*c*.500 CE) of *Visuddhimagga* ("Path to Purity"), which formalised teaching of Theravada (*q.v.*) school. Name, meaning "Voice of the Buddha", is also that of other Buddhist commentators.

Channa Prince Siddhartha's charioteer and companion.

Devadatta One of Prince Siddhartha's cousins, and one of his rivals for the hand of Yasodhara. Subsequently a member of the Sangha (*q.v.*), he conspired to get the Buddha killed.

Dhamma, or Dharma The teaching of the Buddha. Also, Law.

Dhammapada 423-stanza Buddhist canonical work. Word means Path of the Teaching.

Dravidians People inhabiting the south of the Indian subcontinent.

Dukkha Suffering, misery, pain, unhappiness. Along with Anicca (*q.v.*) and Anatta (*q.v.*), is one of three "Signs of Being".

Gautama Family name of the Buddha. Also Gotama.

Gotami, Kisa Kshatriya (*q.v.*) maiden who played a role in Prince Siddhartha's "Great Renunciation". Gotami is also the name of any woman belonging to the Gotama (Sanskrit: Gautama) family.

Guru A religious teacher who takes pupils.

Harappa Early town in northwest of Indian subcontinent. *See also* Mohenjo-Dara.

Hinayana The "small vehicle" of salvation. The term invented by Northern Buddhists of the Mahayana (*q.v.*) school to characterise the Southern school. *See also* Theravada.

Hindu From Persian *hindu*, "land of the great river". Root of "India".

Hinduism Western term for religion of India, preceded by Brahmanism.

Indra An important Brahman and early Indo-European god.

Japiti, Lady Or, Mahaprajapati. Sister of Lady Maya (*q.v.*) and, like her, wife to King Suddhodhana, thus aunt of Prince Siddhartha.

Kamma "King of passions", demon unleashed by Mara (*q.v.*)

Kantaka Name of Prince Siddhartha's white stallion.

Karma Law of continuing effect of one's deeds, inseparable from doctrine of rebirth. Roughly, law of cause and effect.

Kondanna Eldest of the five monks who became the first bhikkhus (*q.v.*), or members of the Sangha (*q.v.*), the Buddhist monastic order. The other four: Assaji, Bhaddiya, Mahanama, Vappa.

Kshatriyas Rulers and warriors, ranking second-highest in Indian caste system (under priests, or Brahmans).

Mahakassapa Buddhist monk who convened First Buddhist Council after the death of the Buddha. Is said to have had the "most precious treasure" of Zen "turned over" to him by the Buddha.

Mahaprajapati Alternative designation of the Buddha's aunt, the Lady Japiti (*q.v.*).

Mahasangiti Faction splitting at Second Buddhist Council and forming the basis of other factions. Believed to be forerunner of Mahayana (*q.v.*) school.

Mahayana Literally, the "great vehicle", comprising the Northern school of Buddhism, which deifies Buddha and has many forms and branches. Now prevalent in China, Korea, Japan, Tibet and Mongolia. *See also* Mahasangiti.

Mahinda Buddhist monk, son of King Asoka (*q.v.*) who, together with his sister, brought Buddhism to Ceylon (now Sri Lanka).

Mano Demon unleashed by Mara (*q.v.*), called "Fiend of Pride".

Mara Deity representing death and evil. The tempter.

Maya Illusion.

Maya-Diva, Lady Mother of Prince Siddhartha Gautama. One of two wives of King Suddhodana (*q.v.*).

Mohenjo-Dara Early town in northwest of Indian subcontinent. See also Harappa.

Nanda One of Prince Siddhartha's rivals for the hand of Yasodhara.

Nirvana Also, Nibbana (Pali). Supreme goal of Buddhism. State of supreme enlightenment. "Reality seen face to face."

Parinirvana Final or complete Nirvana (*q.v.*).

Patigha Demon unleashed by Mara (*q.v.*), representing Hate.

Pitakas Literally, "baskets" holding the teaching. The three Pitakas comprising the Pali Canon: the *Sutta P.* (sermons), the *Vinaya P.* (or rules of the Sangha) and the *Abhidhamma*, containing the Buddha's system of mind-training.

Rahula Son born to Prince Siddhartha and Yasodhara. Name signifies "bond", "tie", "impediment".

Rama Hindu god who, with his half-brothers, collectively made up incarnation of god Vishnu. Hero of *Ramayana*, Sanskrit epic.

Rishi Ascetic who has renounced the world. A hermit, seer, or prophet.

Ruparaga Demon unleashed by Mara (*q.v.*), representing "Lust of Days".

Sakya, or Shakya Tribe or people ruled by Suddhodana (*q.v.*).

Sangha The Buddhist monastic order.

Sanskrit Language the Aryans brought to India.

Shakyamuni A title of the Buddha, meaning "Sage of the Shakya (or Sakya) tribe".

Siddhartha Given name of Gautama Buddha, in Sanskrit form. Meaning "He who has reached his goal." Pali variant: Siddhatta.

Signs of The 32 bodily signs (*lakkhana*) of Buddhahood, based on popular beliefs of physical attributes of a "great man" destined to be a universal ruler or a Buddha, vary slightly in different texts. E. J. Thomas (*see Bibliography*) lists them as follows. "He has (1) well-set feet, (2) wheels with a thousand spokes and rim and nave on the soles of his feet, (3) projecting heels, (4) long fingers, (5) soft hands and feet, (6) netted hands and feet, (7) prominent ankles, (8) antelope limbs, (9) when standing or not stooping his hands reach to his knees, (10) the private member is in a sheath, (11) he has a golden colour, (12) soft skin, (13) there is one hair to each pore of the skin, (14) the hairs of the body are black, rising straight and curling to the right, (15) he is very straight of body, (16) he has seven prominences, (17) the front of his

body is like a lion, (18) he has the space between the
shoulders filled out, (19) his height is equal to his
outstretched arms, (20) he has even shoulders, (21) keen
taste, (22) a lion jaw, (23) forty teeth, (24) even teeth, (25) is
not gap-toothed, (26) has very white teeth, (27) a large
tongue, (28) a voice like Brahma and as soft as a cuckoo's,
(29) very black eyes, (30) eyelashes like an ox, (31) white
hair between the eyebrows, and (32) his head is in the shape
of a cap (*unhisasisa*)." The 80 minor marks (*anuvyanjana*)
include having glossy, prominent and copper-colored nails.
The lists of signs is believed to have developed only in the
Christian era and were soon in contention. Buddhaghosa
(*q.v.*) denies Sign 6, even stating that someone with the
"defect" of webbed fingers could not receive ordination.
According to Thomas, "we know that some of [the signs]
were in fact invented from a study of the peculiarities in the
Indian style of images."

Silabbat-paramasa Demon unleashed by Mara (*q.v.*),
representing Scruple.

Simhahanu Prince Siddhartha's grandfather.

Suddhodana Father of Prince Siddhartha Gautama. Ruler, or
King, of Sakyas (*q.v.*).

Sudras Members of lowest caste in Indian caste system, below
Vaisyas (*q.v.*), but above out-castes (Panchamas).

Sutta (Sanskrit: Sutra) A sermon of (or discourse by) the Buddha.
Literally, a thread on which jewels (teachings) were strung.

Tantra A school of Hinduism which influenced certain Buddhist
schools, as in the Tantric Buddhism of Tibet.

Tapussa Name of one of two merchants who became the
Buddha's first lay followers.

Tathagata A title of the Buddha, used by his followers and by
himself. Meaning uncertain. May mean "He who has
attained his goal", "The Perfect One", "He who follows in
the footsteps of his predecessors", or even "Coming from
no place and going to no place".

Theravada The doctrine of the "Elders" (*Thera*) of the Southern
school of Buddhism and the sole surviving school of the
Hinayana (*q.v.*), the earliest school of Buddhism. Now
prevalent in Sri Lanka (Ceylon), Thailand and Burma. It is
the "small vehicle" of salvation, as contrasted to the "large
vehicle", the Mahayana (*q.v.*).

Uddaka Ramaputta Brahamanic guru and one of Gautama's
teachers.

Uddhachcha Demon unleashed by Mara (*q.v.*), representing Self-
Righteousness.

Upanishads Metaphysical dialogues, written after the Vedas (*q.v.*)
and partly a commentary on them.

Vaisyas Members of merchant caste, ranking just below
Kshatriyas (*q.v.*).

Vedas Aryan Sanskrit legends, becoming Hindu holy books.

Visikitcha Demon unleashed by Mara (*q.v.*), representing Doubt.

Viswamitra Guru or teacher of Prince Siddhartha.

Yasa Young man of Benares who became seventh member of the
Sangha (*q.v.*), as well as an arahant.

Yasodhara Wife of Prince Siddhartha, mother of Rahula. Also
referred to as Gopa Yasodhara.

Yoga Literally, *"yoke"* (that which unites). A school of Hindu
philosophy marked by meditative practices and physical
postures.

Yogi (or Yogin) One who practices Yoga.

Zen Name of a school of Japanese Buddhism. The direct
approach to reality, transcending the intellect. Adaptation of
Chinese *Ch'an*, itself a corruption of the Indian *Dhyana*,
signifying mystic state of serene contemplation attained in
meditation.

Bibliography

Arnold, Sir Edwin, *The Light of Asia*, or *The Great Renunciation* (N.Y.: A. L. Burt Co., 1879)

Babbitt, Irving, transl., *The Dhammapada*: Translated from the Pali with an Essay on Buddha and the Occident (N.Y.: Oxford University Press, 1936; N.Y.: New Directions, 1965)

Bahn, A. J., *Philosophy of the Buddha* (Colliers, 1958)

Ballou, Robert O., ed., *The Bible of the World* (N.Y.: Viking, 1939)

————. *The Portable World Bible* (N.Y.: Viking Press, Viking Portable Library, 1944, 7th. ed. 1958)

Batchelor, Stephen, *The Awakening of the West: The Encounter of Buddhism and Western Culture* (London: Harper Collins Aquarian, 1994)

Bary, William Theodore de, *Sources of Indian Tradition* (N.Y.: Columbia University Press, 1958)

Blyth, R. H., *Zen in English Literature* (N.Y.: Evergreen, 1948)

Boisselier, Jean, *The Wisdom of the Buddha* (London: Thames and Hudson, 1994)

Brewster, E. H., *The Life of Gotama the Buddha* (N.Y.: 1926)

Burtt, Edwin A., ed., *The Teachings of The Compassionate Buddha* (N.Y.: New American Library of World Literature, Inc., a Mentor Book, 1955)

Carus, Dr. Paul, *Dharma* (Open Court)

Cheney, Sheldon, *Men Who Have Walked With God* (N.Y.: Alfred A. Knopf, 1945, rev. ed., 1956)

Conze, Edward, *Buddhism: Its Essence and Development* (N.Y.: Harper & Row, a Harper Torchbook, 1959)

————. ed., *Buddhist Texts Through the Ages* (N.Y.: Harper & Row, a Harper Torchbook, 1964)

Dechanet, J.-M., O.S.B., *Christian Yoga* (N.Y.: Harper & Bros., 1960)

Gard, Richard A., ed., *Buddhism* (N.Y.: Washington Square Press, 1961, new ed. 1963)

Grant, Francis, *Oriental Philosophy, The Story of the Teachers of the East* (N.Y.: Dial Press, 1936)

Goddard, Dwight, ed., *A Buddhist Bible*. rev. & enlgd. ed. (N.Y.: E. P. Dutton & Co., 1938)

Herold, Ferdinand A., *The Life of the Buddha* (Tuttle)

Hirose, Nobuko, ed. & transl. *Immovable Wisdom: The Art of Zen Strategy, the Teachings of Takuan Soho* (Shaftesbury, Dorset, U.K.: Element Books, 1992)

Humphreys, Christmas, *Buddhism* (London: Penguin Books, 1951)

———. *A Buddhist Student's Manual* (London: Buddhist Society, 1956)

———. *Exploring Buddhism* (London: George Allen & Unwin Ltd., 1974)

Jennings, J. G., ed. & transl., *The Vedantic Buddhism of the Buddha* (London: Geoffrey Cumberlege, Oxford University Press, 1948)

Loon, Hendrik Willem van, *The Story of Mankind* (N.Y.: Pocket Books Inc., 1957 ed.)

Malalasekera, G. P., and K. N. Jayatelleke, *Buddhism and the Race Question* (Unesco, 1958)

Mueller, F. Max, transl., *The Dhammapada* (Chicago, Rajput Press, 1911)

———. ed., *Buddhist Suttas* (Oxford: Clarendon Press, 1881; N.Y.: Dover Publications Inc. 1969)

Percheron, Maurice, *The Marvellous Life of Buddha* (N.Y.: St Martin's Press, 1960)

Rahula, Walpola, *What the Buddha Taught* (Evergreen)

Ramacharaka, Yogi, *The Inner Teachings of the Philosophies and Religions of India* (Chicago: Yogi Publication Society 1909, 1936)

Rhys Davids, D. W. (transl.), *Buddhist Suttas*, translated from the Pali (N.Y.: Dover Publications Inc., 1969)

Schumann, H. W., *The Historical Buddha* transl. by M. O'C.
  Walshe (London: Penguin Arkana 1982)
Senzaki, Nyogen, and Ruth McCandless, *Buddhism and Zen*
  (Wisdom Library 1953)
Spear, Percival, *India, a Modern History* (Ann Arbor: University of
  Michigan Press, 1961)
Stryk, Lucien, ed., *World of the Buddha: A Reader* (N.Y.:
  Doubleday Anchor Books, 1969)
Suzuki, Beatrice Lane, *Mahayana Buddhism*, with a foreword by
  Christmas Humphreys, president, Buddhist Society,
  London (Colliers, 1948)
Suzuki, Daisetz Teitaro, *Essays in Zen Buddhism*, with an Editor's
  Foreword by Christmas Humphreys (London: Rider & Co.
  1950)
———. *Zen Buddhism*, ed. by William Barrett (N.Y.: Doubleday
  1956)
———. *On Mahayana Buddhism*, ed. & introduced by Edward
  Conze (N.Y.: Harper & Row, a Harper Torchbook, 1968)
Thomas, Edward Joseph, *The Life of Buddha as Legend and
  History* (London: Routledge and Kegan Paul, 1927;
  paperback, 1975). Contains an extensive Bibliography,
  useful to the advanced student, pages 279–288.
Warren, Harry Clarke, *Buddhism in Translations* (Harvard
  University Press, 1896; N.Y.: Atheneum, 1963)
Watts, Alan W., *An Outline of Zen Buddhism* (London: Golden
  Vision Press, 1932)
———. *The Way of Zen* (N.Y.: Pantheon Books, 1957)
———. *The Spirit of Zen* (London: John Murray, 1936; 3rd ed.,
  1958)
———. *Beat Zen, Square Zen, and Zen* (San Francisco: City Lights
  Books, 1959)

Index